An English Country Manner

More true stories from a Suffolk country estate

RORY CLARK

Constable • London

Constable & Robinson Ltd
55-56 Russell Square
London WC1B 4HP

www.constablerobinson.com

This paperback edition published by Robinson,
an imprint of Constable & Robinson Ltd, 2013

A copy of the British Library Cataloguing in
Publication Data is available from the British Library

ISBN 978-1-78033-899-6

Printed and bound in the EU

1 3 5 7 9 10 8 6 4 2

To Harriet and Jemima

Acknowledgements
To Hal Norman for proving that editors are part human
and to Ruth Tott for her publisher's confidence.

Chapter 1

Sophie's father's nose was orange. Normally it reminded me of distinguished Roman emperors but now a clown came to mind. He peered at me enduringly, his half-moon spectacles further drawing attention to his plumed proboscis.

'What are you doing here, James?' he asked. 'Isn't it bad luck?'

'I've called in to look at the flowers,' I explained. 'I see you've been sniffing them.'

'What?'

'Your nose is orange.'

'Bugger,' he said, taking a spotted handkerchief from his breast pocket. 'Damn lilies I suppose.'

'And it's not bad luck,' I continued, 'I think that refers to seeing the bride in her wedding dress.'

'Oh, does it? I knew there was some sort of nonsense along those lines. You all right? No last-minute qualms?'

He put his arm around my shoulder.

'I've never been so certain of anything in all my life,' I assured him.

There was a pause. 'It must seem strange for you, your only daughter fleeing the nest.'

'It is,' he confirmed, 'but Deirdre and I are very fond of you, as you know, and we are delighted. We totally support the two of you.'

'I promise,' I said, a lump rising in my throat, 'to look after her. Sophie is the most precious person on earth to me and I won't let her down.'

'I know that,' he assured me. 'I have faith in you, that the two of you will succeed.'

He tightened his grip in a manly gesture of comradeship as if to emphasise his convictions.

'You've still got a bit on your left nostril,' I pointed out, breaking the solemnity of the moment.

'I hope the bloody stuff comes off,' he said, having another wipe with his hanky. 'Can't give my daughter away with an orange nose.'

The church door opened, the heavy iron latch crashing like a pistol shot in the silence of the empty stone building. We turned to see who it was coming in. It was the rector.

'Hallo,' he shouted, the lilt of his Irish accent echoing clearly in the vaulted chancel. 'Who is there?'

'Ah, Rector,' replied Sophie's father, 'it's just James and me having a look round before tomorrow.'

'Who? I can't see in this gloom. Wait, I'll come closer.'

Mr O'Reilly had many qualities but a good memory was not among them so it was no surprise that he had forgotten who we were. I only hoped that he would remember to turn up tomorrow although Sophie's father had assured me that the promise of a plentiful supply of whisky at the reception should be enough to guarantee his presence.

'Oh, it's you now there, Mr Cavendish, be decked so you be. And who is this young man?'

'James Aden – you're marrying him tomorrow to my daughter, Sophie, Mr O'Reilly. Surely you remember him. You've met often enough.'

The rector stared at me as if I had just arrived from another planet.

'Oh, yes, forgive me. Now I remember. I thought you looked familiar right enough, to be sure. And where's the gorgeous girl herself, not getting in a panic I trust?'

'No, she's fine I think,' replied Mr Cavendish. 'Doing the usual woman's thing – getting organised I suppose. Worrying about her hair or shaving her legs, something like that!'

'It's a big day for the lass, to be sure. She'll want to look her best, though God himself knows she's blessed with a beauty that doesn't need any painting.'

At least he'd remembered something, I thought, thankfully. The day wouldn't be a total surprise to him.

'Anyway, I've got to get on home,' said Mr Cavendish, 'still things to do for the reception.'

'You will be there, won't you, Mr O'Reilly?'

'Oh, to be sure, Mr Cavendish,' he replied. 'I'm not one to miss a good party now, am I?'

We went on our separate ways, Sophie's father to join his family, me to join mine, including my brother, who was to act as my best man on the morrow and my chaperone for the evening. The two families would dine independently and meet at the church in the morning.

The next day dawned bright, sunny and warm. We were fortunate and thankful for it made everything so much more enjoyable for everyone, especially at a country wedding. The church looked wonderful in the spring sunshine, the scent of newly mown grass giving the promise of heady summer days not far off and the appropriate optimism of a new season beginning.

My brother and I stood at the church porch welcoming guests, whilst several close friends and Harry, Sophie's younger brother, carried out their ushering duties inside. Harry had been enjoying his gap year in Australia when we announced our engagement but had reluctantly agreed to return home when his parents offered to pay for a return flight. He had caused a bit of a stir arriving with bright green hair, decreeing that it was all the rage 'down under'. The contrast with his formal morning tailcoat was certainly striking.

Of course I only knew about half the guests but I had met one or two of the Cavendish family. In particular I remembered Sophie's uncle William Cavendish, her father's bachelor brother. We had visited him at his farm in Suffolk shortly after our engagement. Sophie was his favourite niece and he had insisted that she introduced me to him at the earliest opportunity.

'Good morning, James,' he greeted me. 'The luckiest man alive, eh! Looking forward to it I hope.'

'Hallo,' I replied with a genuinely welcoming smile. 'Yes, can't wait now to get on with it all and start our married lives.'

'You're lucky,' he continued. 'Never found the right one myself. Good luck.'

He walked on into the church and left me reflecting upon our stay at Cordwainers Hall, his charming home in the wilds of East Anglia. Sophie's father had inherited the family farm and his younger brother William had been bought the one in Suffolk when Henry Cavendish had married Sophie's mother. It had given each of the brothers the freedom of independence but it was sad that William had never married. Living alone but for an ageing housekeeper in a grand but decaying house, there were two things that could be said of him with certainty: one, he was eccentric and two, he was immeasurably content with his lot. The place, I recalled, was stuffed with beautiful antique furnishings, all protected, as he put it, by a thick coat of dust and dog hair.

We had eaten what seemed an exotic stew on our first visit. I had thought nothing more of it until the housekeeper had come in afterwards with a message for Mr Cavendish.

"E gorn out then?' she'd muttered, two yellow teeth protruding over her bottom lip.

'Yes, Mrs Painter,' Sophie had told her, 'he's checking a ewe that should have lambed. Is there a message?'

'Tell 'im I've found t'sock he was after. 'E swore it were on the drying rack 'bove t'aga an' I daresay it was. It were in t' bottom of the soup stock. I've rinsed it out for 'im.'

We had visited several times since then as Sophie and William were particularly fond of each other. He seemed to regard her as the daughter that he'd never have and delighted in her interest in his farm and the sheep flock. The meals were always of a similar taste but as neither of us ever suffered any after-effects, whatever happened to have fallen in it that week must at least have been well boiled.

He had offered the use of his house for our wedding reception but when Lord Leghorn had said we could hold the ceremony in the private church on the Rumshott estate we had accepted with grace as there were advantages in holding the event near our home even though we would soon be moving to Viscount Rumshott's estate in Scotland. I arranged for a marquee to be put up at my rented farm in Harbottle for the party following the ceremony.

More people were arriving including a great aunt of mine who stuck in my mind as having sent me an 'I Spy' book on trains for my 22nd birthday. It was interesting who turned up for a wedding, all the distant friends and relatives normally relegated to the Christmas card list. Still, it made for a good mix of people for the party afterwards.

The church was gradually filling up and Stuart and I made our way to the front pew to sit next to my parents. I began to feel nervous, partly about being the centre of attention and partly fearing Sophie might have a last-minute change of mind. She was, without doubt, a great catch and I often wondered what on earth she saw in me.

Mr O'Reilly had been fussing around at the back of the church, in between welcoming the guests in a highly affectionate manner. No doubt he had already had a dram or two in anticipation of the excitement to follow. He came bustling down towards us and dispelled my doubts.

'The bride's here, by deck she is, and what a glorious sight to behold,' he informed me. 'I'll meet her at the church door and then be back to you right enough.'

He rushed away to meet Sophie and her father and the organist, alerted by the goings-on, startled everyone with a sudden blast on the organ. Within a few moments it began vaguely to resemble Vidor's 'Wedding March' and then Sophie entered on the arm of her father, accompanied by her trail of bridesmaids.

It was very moving and I was thankful that Mrs Cavendish wasn't the sort to start weeping. An elegant, striking looking woman, very much in command of her surroundings, she was enjoying her pivotal role in the proceedings. Harry's green hair rather clashed with her dress but that was beside the point.

I turned to look at Sophie walking down the aisle. She looked radiant. A stunning looking girl at any time, she appeared so flawless, so incredibly beautiful that it took my breath away. Even the congregation standing to greet her seemed mesmerised by her beauty. Her smile, the confident walk and assurance reminded me of the evening we had spent together in a rowing boat in the Scottish Highlands, when I had proposed. I had been convinced then that she was the one for me and now she was about to become my wife. The whole thing seemed so fantastical that I barely dared to believe it was real. She was dressed in an exquisite ivory wedding dress, embroidered with pearls. The veil covering her face was delicate enough not to hide her vibrant blue eyes which were alight with excitement and a hint of amusement. She smiled at me when she reached my side, a devastatingly disarming smile that made my heart reach out to her. We stood together at the front of the nave as the congregation belted out the joyous hymn, 'Praise, My Soul, the King of Heaven'.

Apart from repeatedly calling me David, Mr O'Reilly performed quite well. His earlier tot of whisky had taken a hold and although a little forgetful he exuberantly embraced the occasion.

'Do you tek this man to be your wife?' he asked Sophie.

'I'll take him as my husband,' she corrected him.

'Of course I mean to say husband,' he said, flustered. 'Do you tek this man to be your husband?'

'I do.'

'And you, David . . .'

'James,' I reminded him.

'What's that?'

'My name's James.'

'Oh, by goodness, I mean James. Do you, James, tek this woman as your wife?'

Bit by bit we got through the proceedings with a certain amount of amusement rippling through the congregation. Mr O'Reilly unwittingly infused the solemnity of the vows with a light-hearted air, which coincidentally reflected the attitude with which Sophie and I approached our lives.

The generosity of Sophie's parents allowed us to have a really glamorous party, even if it did fly by in a few short hours. There didn't seem to be enough time to talk to people that we knew, let alone the ones we only recognised by name. A blur of reception line, speeches, toasts and wedding cake took us suddenly to our send-off to begin our honeymoon. Our destination was not a secret. A friend of my mother's had offered us the use of her log cabin in the Canadian Rocky Mountains and we had jumped at the chance. Neither of us was the type to sit on a beach and there were plenty of energetic pursuits that appealed to us in Alberta. We enjoyed a blissful two weeks utterly content to be on our own, selfishly thinking of no one but ourselves and what we wanted to do that particular day. The real world and all the changes that would inevitably need to be made for our lives together could wait until we returned.

Apart from the delight of enjoying our first real time together, unfettered by the routine of normal everyday life, we explored the wilderness of the Rockies with an enthusiasm matched only by a spaniel let loose in a shooting covert. We hiked, wary of bears sleepily emerging from a winter's hibernation; we fished for trout in some of the purest fresh waters in the world; we rode out with cattle hands on a ranch; and of course we consummated the love that we had for each other. The isolated log cabin was our own private Eden. We lit a log fire each evening and relaxed in front of its roaring flames, talking and laughing late into the night. With no pressure of time at some point we would slip into the massive old-fashioned bed draped with a heavy patchwork counterpane and curl up, the dim yellow glow of candlelight illuminating the rough-hewn log walls. The intense physical passion that we had experienced at the beginning of our relationship hadn't lessened, moreover it had deepened to a constant suppressed desire.

Sophie's arresting beauty continued to catch me unawares. No matter how much time we spent together, every so often

I would suddenly be reminded of her sensuality, the overt sexual aura that surrounded her and made her so irresistible. She didn't seem to be aware of the effect that she had on me, or the other men who so often looked admiringly in her direction. Her tall, slim body helped of course, and her long dark hair and striking blue eyes added to the finely shaped lines of her face with its prominent cheekbones, but there was something else too. Something that was difficult to define. A presence of confidence and happiness perhaps.

Looking back to when Sophie had first arrived at the Rumshott estate office as an assistant, and the tortuous path that our relationship had followed, it seemed incredible that we were now married. All the decisions I had made, all the work I had done and all the efforts I had made were now for a purpose, the goal of our shared happiness. It made everything more worthwhile.

When we returned home there was a lot to do. Although my brother had very kindly arranged for the mess left by the wedding party to be cleared up that was the least of our worries. Apart from moving house we had to arrange the sale of the stock on my rented farm. It was not possible to take the lowland sheep up to the Highlands as they'd never thrive and besides, we did not have the opportunity of renting a farm up there. The sale was arranged a week after our return from Canada and the fortnight abroad disappeared in a haze of distant memories.

Within a month I would finish working as the deputy agent for Earl Leghorn at Rumshott and we would move up to the Glen Arrin estate where I had been offered the job as factor, or land agent, for Viscount Rumshott, the earl's son. It was an exciting opportunity and one that both Sophie and I were looking forward to immensely.

Our first priority was to organise the farm sale. It was

sad to see everything go having spent the previous four years building it all up. I was leaving behind a lovely house with many happy memories, a quality sheep flock that I had bred myself and of course all the people that we had got to know on the estate. But we had no qualms. The possibilities and the promotion of moving to the Highlands outweighed the comfortable option of staying put.

We woke early on the day of the sale. The dead stock, machinery, equipment and bits and pieces were already laid out in rows in the field, but the sheep had to be gathered and sorted into the temporary pens to be sold in lots according to their age and condition. My border collie, Jess, was in heaven with all the work to do and of course had no idea that it would be the last time she'd be rounding up sheep for me. After the sale she was going to Sophie's uncle and sad as I was to see her go, I did not agree with keeping a working dog as a pet.

Brian Cattermole, the auctioneer, arrived as we were penning the last few lambs. A jolly rotund fellow with a large red face, he had got his trade down to an art form. His love of a farm sale and the accompanying gossip was legendary in the area and brought far more people than just those interested in buying something on offer.

'Got 'em all in then, James?' he asked.

'Yup, I think everything's just about ready. Have a look round and then come in for a cup of tea,' I suggested.

'Good idea, lad,' he said. 'Want to meet this cracking new wife I hear you've got!' He wandered towards the field gate. 'I'll be over in a minute.'

Sophie was in the kitchen on the telephone to her mother. I put the kettle on the Aga.

'Brian Cattermole's here,' I mouthed. 'He's coming in for a cup of tea.'

She finished her conversation and put the phone down. 'Apparently, Uncle William's coming over to the sale,' she said excitedly.

'Oh,' I replied, 'he didn't say anything when we last spoke. I was going to take Jess over there next week.'

'He's only just decided. Dad says it's because he wants to see how good or not our sheep are!'

'Perhaps he'll buy some.'

There was a knock on the door. 'Hallo,' shouted Mr Cattermole, sticking his head round. 'Can I come in?'

'Of course. Meet Sophie.'

They introduced themselves as I filled the teapot.

'Is everything okay out there?' I asked, hoping that we wouldn't have to start changing things around. There wasn't much time before the sale would begin.

'It's all in great shape,' he assured me. 'And I must say the sheep are looking fit. We'll be bound to get a good price on them.'

Good for the current values, I thought, but with the state farming was in I doubted that I would be particularly pleased.

We heard some vehicles arriving and hastily finished our tea.

'Come on, we'd better get started,' chortled Mr Cattermole, 'there'll be a whole load of gossip to catch up on before we get underway.'

We traipsed outside to greet the early arrivals. Some Sophie and I knew from our work on the estate but more and more strange faces appeared. And there were some strange faces. I often wondered how the farming community could produce such a huge mixture of types all under the one umbrella. There was Colonel Dambridge, a tall, distinguished-looking man dressed in a tweed suit who farmed at Priory Farm, an impeccable place on the edge of the estate; Mr Sparkes, my neighbour, a miserable sort of fellow who saw gloom in every eventuality; and a group of gypsy types looking with extraordinary interest at a heap of scrap metal and accompanied by a gaggle of large buxom women puffing cheap cigarettes. But by and large the gathering consisted of a lot of cheery, enthusiastic livestock farmers enjoying a day out.

By the time Brian was ready to start the sale, the field beside the driveway was jam-packed with a huge variety of vehicles. A sizeable, expensive-looking Mercedes which belonged to one of the local sheep dealers was surrounded by lorries, Land Rovers and even a few tractors. Several cars looked as though this was their final resting place although I suspected that through the dexterity of their owners' skills with bits of string, wire and curses all save one or two would depart as planned.

My boss, the agent at Rumshott, George Pratt, had arrived to lend his support and was chatting to Sophie. I walked over to join them next to the sheep pens.

'Ah, morning, James,' he boomed, his greeting startling the ewes in the adjoining pen. 'Looks like a good turnout for you, I'm pleased to see. Don't want to give anything away to these rogues. Need a bit of competition.'

'There seems to be plenty of that,' I agreed, looking around the sale field. 'Quite surprising really, after all it's only a small sale.'

'Part of it's because it's Rumshott, I expect,' George said, staring intently at me. 'Are you still sure about your decision to take on this Scottish estate? No last-minute doubts? Giving all this up for a few thousand acres of peat bog, 364 days a year of rain and a load of natives who think a cultured night out means getting pissed and tossing logs.'

George had never been entirely supportive of either Viscount Rumshott's purchase of Glen Arrin, or my intention to manage it. Sophie butted in. 'I don't think you really know Scotland, George,' she said. 'It is full of the most amazing opportunities for those who bother to look. And it's unspoilt, beautiful and wild.'

'I have been there,' George exclaimed indignantly. 'I spent the wettest, coldest, most uncomfortable week of my life there sharing a tent with a school pal and about a quarter of a million midges.'

'Ah well,' Sophie concluded, 'if you would just give it a second chance then maybe you would see it differently.'

'You'll have to visit us,' I offered, 'but now, if you'll excuse me I want to listen to the bidding.'

Brian had started off with the small items: hand tools, veterinary equipment, hay racks and so on. I was more concerned about the farm machinery and the sheep. That was where most of the value lay. As we listened, we were inevitably disappointed by some prices yet pleased with others. All in all the sale proved to be reasonably successful. I was particularly delighted when Uncle William bought fifty of my best ewe tegs to take back to Suffolk. At least I would be able to see some of the results of my home-bred progeny develop.

Chapter 2

Sophie had finished working in the estate office just before our wedding and, having aborted plans to study estate management at Cirencester, was considering enrolling at a college in Inverness to take a degree in forestry. The intention was that she would take on the responsibility of the sizeable Glen Arrin forest enterprise in due course. Meanwhile I still had some projects to finish off at Rumshott before we left and George, suddenly realising that he was about to be bereft of a deputy, hastily advertised for a replacement in the professional magazines.

He wanted; me to sit in on the first round of interviews and the short-listed would then be seen by Lord Leghorn and Viscount Rumshott. I didn't see that I could be much help. I wouldn't be working with them and George's priorities when presented with the candidates were unpredictable.

'I thought that chap was good,' I said to him as we watched one hopeful walk back across the stableyard to his car. 'Had some useful experience, technically knowledgeable . . .'

'Look at the way he's shuffling,' barked George, interrupting me. 'Bloody shuffling along like a cow with mastitis, banging its tits against its hocks.'

'I beg your pardon?'

'Look,' he pointed out of the window. I had to admit the chap wasn't exactly striding out but one could hardly call it shuffling.

'Well, I don't think you can discard him just for that,' I said.

'You can tell a great deal by the way a man walks,' he replied. 'More important than what he knows about landlord and tenant law. You can teach him that but his walk, well that sums up his attitude to life. His whole *raison d'être*.'

Hoping that some of the other interviewees due in that day would be more to George's liking, I slipped back into my own office to get on with the final odds and ends in readiness for my departure. My involvement with the interviews was an unnecessary hindrance, in my view.

The earl, like George, didn't seem to grasp the fact that I was leaving shortly and trying to get things wrapped up quickly. A continuous trickle of messages landed on my desk from his lordship, all of which he deemed to be of the utmost importance.

'His lordship rang,' said Louise, our secretary. 'Wants you to pop over to the house straightaway.'

'Oh, damn. What's it about this time?' I asked her.

'Haven't a clue.'

I walked over to the house, taking time to delight in the magnificence of the gardens. Hawthorne, the gardener, was chugging away methodically on his lawnmower in the distance, leaving perfect striped patterns on the lawns which stretched to the imposing south front of Rumshott House. The early April sunshine bathed the countryside in light and warmth and I felt momentarily how much I would miss this place. Its atmosphere reeked of stability and wealth, of grandeur and perfection. Scotland would be different, still magnificent in its own way but more rugged around the edges and harsher in both climate and setting.

I tapped in the security combination at the back door and

let myself in. The staff quarters were deserted. I made my way through the maze of corridors to the green baize door that opened into the formal part of the East Wing where his lordship's study was situated. There was a commotion going on inside and I could hear the countess' raised voice.

'I really cannot see the point of getting a cat,' she stormed. 'You know how I loathe animals, Henry. It's a stupid idea. Just get these pest control people, whoever they are, to do a proper job and we won't get any more trouble.'

'I th-thought it could live in the cellars,' his lordship replied. 'You'd n-never see it.'

I knocked on the door and walked through. Lady Leghorn spun round.

'Who is it? Oh, James, what do you want?'

'Good morning, Lady Leghorn,' I replied, anxious not to embark on a contentious discussion with her. 'Lord Leghorn asked me to come over.'

'I'm sure it can wait. I'm in the middle of a very important meeting with his lordship, can't you see? And I'm not to be interrupted.'

'N-no, it's all right,' he said to me, 'come in. It's all a-about the same th-thing.'

'What do you mean, Henry? Is James involved with this cat idea?'

'Well s-sort of.'

This was news to me. I'd never heard the earl express any particular affection for cats and the last thing I needed was to become embroiled in one of their domestic disputes.

'Sort of what? We do not want a cat in this house,' her ladyship insisted.

'I asked J-James to come over so that he could order the cat,' he explained. 'I've got a book here sh-showing all the d-different breeds. I expect you know the best type to get as a mouser, d-don't you, J-James?' He gesticulated vaguely at a glossy book on his desk, entitled *All You Ever Wanted to Know About Cats*.

'We're not having a bloody cat. James, I don't think there's any point in you staying. His lordship's mind has changed.'

'Oh,' I said hesitantly. 'Perhaps there's something else we can do. Is there a mouse problem that I haven't been told about?'

'Apparently. I haven't been told either,' Lady Leghorn snorted.

'It w-wasn't anything that w-would have c-concerned you, d-dear. There are mice in my claret cellar. Thousands of them. I th-think they're immune t-to the poison being laid,' he explained.

'Well, perhaps it would be simpler, my lord, to get a different type of poison. I'll speak to the pest people we have a contract with. They must encounter this all the time.'

'Please do that immediately,' said the countess. 'And if they can't sort it out then fire them. Get someone else. Under no circumstances, d'you hear me, are we having a cat.'

'Very well. I'll ring them this morning and report back to you with the outcome, my lord.'

Perhaps I wasn't going to miss Rumshott after all, I thought as I returned to the estate office. At least Edward, Viscount Rumshott, and his wife Elizabeth, who would be my bosses at Glen Arrin, had a better grip on reality.

I made an appointment for the rat catcher to come out and then joined George in another interview with a prospective replacement for me. I wondered whether this one would be a strider or a shuffler. We didn't get that far.

'Are you seriously telling me,' George was stuttering with undisguised apoplexy, 'that you want two days a week off to hunt? This is a bloody job here, not a flaming hobby.'

'I've always worked on estates where this has been possible before,' lamented the unfortunate candidate. 'I consider it all part of the lifestyle as a resident agent.'

'You consider . . .'

'If I might just butt in,' I interjected, sensing George was about to explode, 'I'll explain why that's not possible here. Frankly there is just too much to do and whilst I occasionally get a day out if they're meeting locally it would be too much to expect more than that. You'd have to accept that.'

The Honourable Giles Church looked crestfallen and mumbled something about perhaps it not being a suitable job for him.

'What's that you're saying?' barked George. 'Can't hear a damn word.'

'I said I think that I had better reconsider the situation,' he repeated.

'I think that would be an excellent idea,' said a clearly annoyed George, standing up to indicate that the interview was already at an end. 'Probably best to find yourself some-where where all they have to worry about is the price of fish.'

So the second candidate departed and we were no further forward.

'Just as well I nipped that one in the bud before we wasted any more time,' remarked George shortly. 'Met that type before. No spine.'

'Well let's hope third time lucky,' I commented. 'What time is the next one due?'

'Four o'clock. Name's Frances Upfront, currently work-ing on a large estate near Oxford, excellent references.'

'Good. Maybe some success will come of it. I'll be back in by then but I'm just nipping home for a bite to eat.'

It seemed strange having Sophie at home when I arrived. I was used to her being in the office rather than preparing lunch.

'How's the packing going?' I asked, aware that she had spent all morning wrapping things up ready for the removal men.

'Fine, thanks. I don't reckon it's going to take as long as I first thought, you know.'

'Oh, well, that's good. I'm worried that moving day will be upon us before we know it. And I've still got loads to finish off in the office.'

I told her about the continuing interruptions which she understood only too well, having experienced them herself over the past two years.

'His lordship didn't really think a single cat would be any use did he? The cellars run for miles, he'd need a dozen to do any good.'

'Well, you know what it's like. Anyway the whole thing was scotched by her ladyship. The thought of an animal in the house freaked her.'

Sophie laughed. 'It's going to be so different at Glen Arrin. Hopefully, you'll be able to concentrate on the estate rather than the trivial everyday hoo-ha's.'

'I hope so too,' I agreed. 'Plus, of course, the Rumshotts won't be there that often. Not like here when the Leghorns are in more or less permanent residence.'

I left Sophie and returned to the office. I desperately wanted to clear my desk within the next week so that Sophie and I could spend time together before leaving for Scotland. I hoped the next interviewee would be more satisfactory.

It started off badly.

'Right,' George said to me in his brusque, businesslike manner, 'this next chap promises to be something. Presently working as an assistant on the Bailythin estate, 12,000 acres, qualified three years ago.'

'Have you got his CV there?' I asked, wanting a quick flick through before the interview.

He began searching through the mountains of papers on his desk. 'Bloody thing's here somewhere, I'm sure,' he muttered.

I rustled around the files nearest me. 'What's this doing here?' I asked, holding up a slice of dried ham that I had found wedged between a letter from the district council and a brochure on Armitage Shanks' lavatories.

'Ah,' he said, 'I wondered where that had gone. Thought it strange that I had a sandwich with no filling. Good ham that too, you know, from old Parker's pig.'

The telephone rang on his desk. 'Yes,' he shouted.

'Frances Upfront is here to see you, Mr Pratt,' informed Louise. 'Shall we come up?'

'Yes, thank you, Louise. Come straight on in.'

There was an unmistakable pause when Miss Frances Upfront was shown in. Frances was, to George's surprise, a woman. He obviously hadn't read her CV clearly. She was also, I happened to notice, upfront in design as well as by name.

'Um, er, do please sit down,' he managed to say. 'I, er, I was expecting um . . . someone not quite so attractive as you. Forgive me. Er, would you like a cup of tea? Louise, some tea for us all I think, please. Earl Grey. And biscuits.'

'I'm afraid there aren't any biscuits, Mr Pratt. You told me they were an extravagance we couldn't afford.'

'Did I? Don't remember saying that.'

'You did, Mr Pratt. Even custard creams were beyond our reach, that was how you put it.'

'Well then,' he smiled warmly at Miss Upfront, 'we'll have to make do with just tea then.'

If our interviewee thought there was anything unusual about her potential employer's behaviour, or a conversation about biscuits bizarre, she certainly covered it well. I did notice her, however, looking quizzically at the slice of ham on the desk.

Considering the misunderstanding over the gender of the applicant, the interview went very well. Well enough, in fact, for George to invite Miss Upfront back for a second round and to meet the earl. I was relieved that we might have found a suitable person to take over from me as it was one less thing for me to worry about. I suspected that his lordship, known to appreciate an attractive woman, would be more influenced by the size of Miss Upfront's front than her impeccable references.

Our final fortnight at Rumshott sped past, filled as it was with tying up loose ends in the office and making farewell visits to our friends on the estate. I also had to fit in a quick visit to Scotland to make some arrangements for our arrival at our estate house in Glen Arrin. Sophie would stay at Harbottle to look after the animals we still had. The sheep had all gone now but Grehan, my horse, and Bramble, my Labrador, we were taking with us. I flew up from Gatwick early one Wednesday, not relishing the thought of the journey. I knew that I would be forced to park in some distant car park surrounded by a high chain-link fence before being catapulted around the perimeter of the airport in an ironically named courtesy bus. I would then have to sit around for hours paying extortionate sums for disgusting cups of tea. Only the thought of my destination would keep me going. Glen Arrin. Glen Arrin. Simply saying the name evoked memories of the wild untamed Highlands, the beauty and solitude of the vast empty spaces stretching as far as one could see in all directions.

The journey itself was uneventful except for the first sight of the great bulk of the mountains lying to the west of Inverness which always stirred me. I drove a hired Land Rover Discovery away from the airport, following the wide Moray Firth towards Inverness, skirted the town itself and took the picturesque road along the Beauly Firth towards the mountains. The sunshine, reflecting off the water, blazed from a brilliant blue sky. The distant mountains were shrouded in a veil of cloud, the desolate emptiness at once comforting and awesome. A further thirty minutes' drive and I was snaking my way along the single track road into the glen, the peaty waters of the River Arrin tumbling alongside. I followed the river for ten miles, until I was amongst the rocky crags of Glen Arrin.

The village itself was small, with maybe twenty houses, a village hall, a disused school and a church. The Victorian lodge stood on a slight knoll overlooking the cluster of stone cottages. I swept up the driveway through a thick bank of rhododendrons to the stable block behind the house. The estate office formed one side of the quadrangle. I spent half a day in the office, which in a way did more harm than good as it made me realise how little I knew about the place. It was a challenge though, rather than a worry and without too much concern I set off to have a look at what would be our home.

The factor's house on the estate was an old manse. Built in 1830 it had some historical interest as it was one of the 'Parliamentary manses' designed by Thomas Telford. He had been commissioned by Parliament in 1823 to design and build 32 churches and 43 manses in remote Highland parishes and one of these had been located in Glen Arrin, apparently 'a particularly remote and needy place'. The house was a single-storey building and had been converted with great care into a comfortable home. The estate had bought it some years previously when a full-time minister was no longer deemed necessary in the glen.

All our furniture and belongings were being brought up from England but I needed to ensure that the new carpets and kitchen appliances were in place and some redecorating had been finished. It was worth the trouble to ensure that we had a good start to our married life. During my brief visit I talked to the various tradesmen and as I left I was confident that all would be ready for our arrival.

Chapter 3

May was a good time of year to arrive in the Highlands. The weather brought a clarity of light and freshness to the glen, the rivers were high, the colours magical. Any lingering doubts about the move were dispelled the moment one walked outside and breathed in the pure invigorating air.

All our belongings had been delivered safely apart from one chair that was now missing a leg which we found several weeks later in a commode. Sophie and I had driven up towing a horse trailer with Grehan in it and Bramble in the car. It had been a slow, boring journey relieved by frequent, generally unpleasant stops in motorway service stations. One of the joys of being located in the wilds of the north was that the chances of having to eat in such a place again were low. They were fine for letting the dog out for a pee or filling up with fuel, but that was it.

On our first morning, Sophie went off to her appointment at Inverness College with a tutor from the forestry faculty. I meanwhile drove down to the estate office. It was a daunting feeling arriving with little clue as to exactly what I was supposed to do. I had the experience and the training and I had been entrusted with the whole affair but there was no factor to break me in. Happily, the staff, both in the office and out on the estate, were old hands at the job so I would be able to rely on them to point me in the right direction. But it was important for me to make a good impression from the start or it would take months of work to rebuild any respect from the local people. Mrs McIver, the secretary, was expecting me.

'Och, there ye are, Mr Aden,' she exclaimed, the resonance of her true Highland accent carrying across the yard. 'And how are ye just now?'

'I'm very well, thank you, Mrs McIver. It's lovely to see you again. And you're well too I hope?' I smiled warmly at her.

We spent a while fiddling around with papers, with me trying to get some idea of what was happening on the estate. Most importantly I wanted to get to know the place a bit better as I found it hard to relate what was going on where.

'You know, Mrs McIver,' I said, 'I'm going to go out for the afternoon and take a look around. I don't want to be stuck in here all day reading files.'

'Och well, Mr Aden,' she trilled, 'I can't say as I blame you for that. You'll need to tek a wee while learning your way around.'

I took the opportunity to go fishing, hiking back into the hills to some hidden lochs rarely frequented by anyone. The area I'd chosen from the map was called Loch nan Dearg, a dour peat brown stretch of water nestling under the towering crags of Sgurr a'Chlaonaidh. I turned to look back down the way I had just climbed.

Miles of peat hags, heather and mulberry criss-crossed trickling burns. They could be a daunting place, the Highlands. Solitude spanned the mountains. Yet the wholeness, the emptiness and the peacefulness, more important than the deer, the fish and the forests, filled my soul with a calm reasoning. It would be a wonderful place to live.

I reached the loch and unpacked my fishing rod. A light

breeze ruffled the water and kept away most of the midges. There had been many times before when I'd stood on the edge of a loch surrounded by a black cloud of the tiny insects. They would find their way on to every inch of bare skin, into one's nose and eyes, occasionally feasting on an ear. Often they were joined by the bigger clegs, easier to brush away or swat but more painful when they bit. That afternoon was blessedly free of them and I could tie a fly to the line unhampered by their evil antics. I chose a blue Zulu, a small blue-and-black fly with a streak of a red tail and cast it well out on to the water. I soon had a small brown trout dancing on the line, as wild and pure a fish as you'd ever find. A few of these, each only a mere six or seven ounces, was enough for the following day's breakfast.

Later I followed a burn back down the mountainside towards the glen road and came across Jock Mackenzie, one of the stalkers. He was checking the pipe that supplied water to his cottage 100 feet below. An incredibly gifted deer stalker he was able to read the minds of the red deer that roamed the hills. Very few people came back from a stalk with Jock unsuccessful in their quest for a deer. But he was as dour as the peat brown lochs of the hills.

He had taken Sophie, me and a small party of others on a stalk during a visit to the estate the previous winter in advance of our move up north. I had thought that I was well prepared for what I knew would be an arduous day on the hill. It had been a bitingly cold morning in December with some new snow on the ground and an icy wind that cut through my thick layers of tweed. I had pulled my cap further down and my coat collar tighter around my neck to keep the warmth in and noticed that Jock didn't seem as affected as myself. The flaps of his deerstalker hat had remained fastened on top, leaving his ears exposed to the ferocious wind.

'Don't you ever let down the flaps of your hat to keep your ears warm,' I asked, not believing that he wasn't feeling the cold.

He shook his head mournfully. 'Nae since t'day o' t'accident,' he replied mysteriously.

We continued to walk determinedly across the frozen heather but after some time it became obvious that he wasn't going to expand on this without further prompting. Wary of bringing up what had evidently been a disastrous day for him I tentatively enquired again.

'You had an accident up on the hill?' I asked.

'Aye, an accident on t'hill,' he confirmed.

We crossed many more yards of ground before he continued.

'It were a day just like this 'un,' he said, the Highland lilt endowing his words with deep melancholy.

'Aye, a cold, cold wind. A wee bit earlier in t'season after t'stags. We was away back beyond Sghurr a Mollin with a party o'Americans after a bonnie stag.'

We had reached some peat hags before he continued, the sadness in his voice plain to hear.

'We'd bin on t'hill for five hours, five gruelling hours. We took t'stag perfectly. A clean shot through t'heart.'

I waited patiently with mounting anticipation through the next period of silence. Perhaps I should never have pursued the question. He was clearly finding the memory very distressing.

'I led t'party o'er t'wee staggie. A royal it were. Twelve points on his 'ead.'

I wondered whether we'd ever reach the end of the tale as the silence stretched put once again.

'An' that's when it happened,' he cried. 'The American took out his flask o'whisky, offered me a dram, and I ne'er heard him.'

He had recounted all this without the slightest trace of humour in his voice. His expression hadn't faltered a bit. Even now, as he looked up from his water pipe, there was not even a flicker of surprise at seeing me. It was as though I passed by every day.

'Hallo, Jock,' I said.

'Och,' he said. 'You're gettin' on all right then?'

'Yes, thank you,' I replied. 'Thought I'd get out and start learning where things are, see what's going on,' I explained.

'Aye.'

'Still it seems as though everything is okay.'

'Aye.' He resumed his inspection of the water pipe and pulled out a dead frog. 'I thought as much,' he commented, as he threw it into the heather.

'That's had it by the look of it,' I said.

'Aye.' More silence.

'Well, I expect I'll see you before too long then, Jock,' I said in farewell.

'Aye,' he replied and went back to the pipe.

Watching Jock deal with his water pipe emphasised the huge differences between Scottish and English estates. In England water came via the mains supply, in Scotland every house had to rely on a nearby stream and to draw on the peaty brown water. Interruptions to the supply were caused by dead frogs rather than workmen digging up the road. The remoteness of the Highlands estate not only meant a lack of basic services but also increased the cost of nearly everything we did. Builders in particular cost more as they tended to spend a quarter of the working day travelling to and from the estate. Deliveries were similarly affected. To offset some of these difficulties the European Commission classed the Highlands as a development area and huge grants were available to support projects in the region. Sadly, but not wholly unsurprisingly, much of the money was spent in true Euro style with no regard for its effectiveness.

The glen lying to the west of Arrin sported a wonderful example. In the midst of a peculiarly gaunt and barren landscape, through which a simple branch road, rarely used, wound its way towards the coast, an enormous roundabout had been built. Presumably there had been a pot of designated roundabout money.

But the inconveniences of living in the remote glens were far outweighed by the opportunities. That evening I returned to the manse and suggested to Sophie that we make a cold supper and row out into the loch for an impromptu picnic. The freedom to be able to go where we wanted, when we wanted, was an irresistible draw to a life in the Highlands.

There was, of course, another element to the attraction. This was the same boat and the same loch on which I had proposed to Sophie. The lapping of the water against the wooden hull and the cry of the oyster catchers took us back to that evening. Then, as now, the mesmerising beauty of the majestic mountains sweeping down to the loch's edge was breathtaking.

'Could you please pass me a pickled egg, Sophie?' After a hard day at work and a meagre lunch I needed some protein.

'Just as long as you don't expect me to kiss you after you've eaten it.' Sophie grimaced at the thought of it and laughed.

We both munched happily in silence as the sun set behind the hills and the water of the loch gurgled around our boat. Sophie's hair moved slightly in the light breeze and she occasionally brushed at it with a spare finger in the same way a horse swishes its tail to rid itself of an irritating fly. She looked stunning and I was filled with pride.

'Isn't this wonderful?' I sighed. 'I can't believe how lucky I am, not only to have you as my wife but to be living somewhere so beautiful.'

Sophie smiled as she reached for another tuna sandwich. It was turning a little chilly now as the sun disappeared and the wind appeared to be picking up.

'I hope we don't get caught in a sudden storm,' she joked. 'In this flimsy excuse for a boat we'd be tossed about like a salad.'

'We'll be fine, don't worry, we're not that far from shore, and the boat is a lot stronger than it looks.' To demonstrate the point I stood up and rocked the boat gently from side to side.

'You see, nothing. And I'm using as much force as I can. A force eight gale could come through here and we'd . . . 'My concentration left me as my foot went through the floor panel of the boat with a loud cracking sound. Sophie shrieked with alarm as cold water gushed through the gaping hole.

'James, you idiot!'

We both frantically filled the hole with anything we could lay our hands on; half a loaf of brown bread did the trick for twenty seconds before it disintegrated. Sophie's idea of covering a large lump of my favourite cheese in tarpaulin and shoving it in the hole had initially been rejected, but now it looked as though that was the only thing which might save us from a very wet return to shore. My beloved dolcelatte, saved for a special occasion, moulded itself into the exact shape of the hole in our boat, and Sophie's face as she squeezed it told me she wished it was some part of my anatomy. I was not only soaking wet from the waist down and starting to shiver but emotionally damaged by this turn of events. I had managed to turn our romantic picnic into a bedraggled farce and my wife was not amused.

'There, that's fixed it temporarily.' She glared at me as we continued baling out water with the plastic cups we'd brought along in our hamper.

'I'm so sorry, Sophie, I had no idea that would happen.' I was now rowing frantically, hoping my expensive cheese would hold tight for a few more minutes.

We arrived back at the shore and Sophie clambered out, wet and cold. I dragged the boat up the small gravel beach and finally threw the hamper on to the grassy bank. With my now pink frozen fingers I clawed at the cheese.

'What are you doing now?' Sophie was in a bad mood.

'I just thought . . .' Now I felt foolish. 'I thought I might be able to save the cheese,' I mumbled into my collar.

'You care more about your stupid rotten cheese than you do about me. I could have drowned out there. I still could catch pneumonia or hypothermia.'

I rushed over and enveloped her in my arms. She was very, very cold and trembling.

'Darling, I love you. Let's go home.'

We got back to the Land Rover where I pulled out a large blanket and wrapped it round Sophie's shoulders. She climbed into the passenger seat and I started the engine.

'James . . .'

'Yes, darling?'

'Go and get the cheese.' She grinned at me.

I jumped out of the vehicle and ran back to the boat. Sophie had clearly forgiven me for being so stupid, and I could rescue my cheese. But as I neared the edge of the loch I was dismayed to see a small black goat inside the boat gnawing at the tarpaulin package. It had evidently smelt the contents and decided they would make a fine feast. The excitement of such a lucky find had prompted a shower of goat droppings, which rather put me off the cheese, and as the animal heard me approach it turned its head towards me and dribbled a massive globule of goat saliva on to the now opened cheese.

I returned to the Land Rover, my shoulders slumped in dejection. Sophie had seen the goat from a distance and guessed at the reason for my depression.

'Never mind, James, we can buy some more.' She tried to sound cheery, knowing full well that this particular cheese had been sent to me from Italy. It had been made according to a family recipe passed down through the centuries, and I was never likely to come across an example of it again. I hadn't even opened the foil covering to sniff the damn thing.

We drove back to the house in silence.

Chapter 4

One Friday evening after we had been in Glen Arrin for about a month, Sophie and I decided to go into Inverness to see a film. Already we had fallen into the Highland ways and the hour's drive to the nearest town seemed quite an expedition. The thought of seeing people out on the streets dressed up for clubbing, eating out or whatever, was exciting. It reminded me of the first days of going out with Sophie when I hardly knew her and the nervous adrenalin buzz set my pulse racing.

We left the glen with its aura of remoteness and solitude and headed over the Kessock Bridge into Inverness. It was busy with not only the Inverness inhabitants on their night out, but also people from the surrounding area. Some travelled as far as 100 miles to spend the evening in town. There were few towns of any size north of here, just mile after mile of desolate emptiness, punctuated every so often by small settlements of rural communities. It was almost as though we were in a frontier town.

Of course Inverness wasn't quite like that. It had many of the national retailers in the High Street, an attractive, modern shopping centre, and plenty of bars and restaurants. There were, after all, a great number of tourists who visited the area. We chose to eat in a cheery Italian restaurant down by the river which led from Loch Ness into the Moray Firth. On the edge of the town, beneath the high mound on which

Inverness Castle stood, the riverside setting was pretty and lively. This was the first time we'd been out properly since our wedding and it felt as though we were on a date again. It was fun. We flirted, behaved like new lovers and sat in the back row of the cinema to watch the film. Later, after a moment of impulsive decision, we danced in Mr G's, Inverness' answer to the Ministry of Sound. The nightclub was packed with energetic revellers and although we were in the far north, the music was up to date with the latest in dance fashion.

The scene was much as you would expect in any nightclub. There was a heaving bar, there were men slouching tight, revealing clothes writhing around on the dance floor exhibiting their mating call. Imagination wasn't necessary. Short dresses and low-cut tops made their own statements. Gyrating hips and pouting lips spoke the same language. Bottles of designer lager and a haze of cigarette smoke bore witness to the dropping of inhibitions.

Sophie, tall, dark and stylishly dressed in a sexy, contour-hugging outfit, drew the inevitable attentions of drunk, leering men lurching across the dance floor like cockroaches heading to their feast. For all that, it was invigorating to taste the suppressed carnal desires of a highly charged atmosphere, the total opposite to our everyday life. Variety was indeed a vital ingredient to an interesting existence.

We stayed until two o'clock in the morning before making our way back to the glen. The stark contrast couldn't have been more marked than when we stepped out of the car at the manse. Sophie shivered slightly and I put my arm around her.

'Ssh,' I said. 'Let's just listen for a moment.'

Around us the dark bulk of the mountains was silhouetted against the night sky and Celid na Moirah, highest of all, loomed forebodingly above the manse. All we could hear was the sound of the burns tumbling down the hills to join the river and a faint whisper of a breeze stroking the heather. Sophie shivered again.

'Are you cold?' I asked her.

'No, not really,' she replied. 'I don't know, something spooked me. Someone walking over my grave I think, you know, sent a shiver down my spine.'

'Shall we go in then?' I suggested.

'In a moment. I love this feeling of being so close to, urn, I suppose creation in a way. They don't frighten me, the mountains or the silence. But they do humble me, make me aware of my own mortality.'

After a while longer, standing in awe of the solitude, we went inside. The Aga in the kitchen pumped out a welcome warmth and Bramble, disturbed from her sleep, gave a few thuds of her tail on the floor without getting up.

'You lazy old thing,' I said to her, stroking her head. 'Sophie, do you want a wee dram before we turn in?'

'Whisky makes you frisky, is that the idea?' she laughed.

'Might be!'

'Go on then. Just a wee one though.'

She came up behind me as I poured the drinks and clutched me in a vice-like grip.

'Did you enjoy tonight?' she asked.

'Yeah, it was great fun,' I replied. 'What about you?'

'Brilliant, yes, we'll have to do it again soon.' She paused. 'What about the club, did you enjoy that?'

'Yes, I did in a funny sort of way. I never think they're the same when you're going out with someone or married. They're really best when you're on the pull I suppose, aren't they?'

'Didn't you fancy any of those girls then, the ones

dancing practically naked, coming up to you squirming suggestively.'

'Well, I wasn't really looking. Some were pretty, in a sexy sort of way, but I've got you haven't I, and I promise you, there was no one sexier or more stunning than you there tonight. Just look at all the blokes you had lusting after you.'

'Did you mind that?'

'Not really,' I said. 'I love you and we've got each other. That's what matters. I know you're not going to do anything and the fact is you're a pretty girl so you'll always get attention.'

Sophie tightened her grip. 'Let's go to bed.'

'That sounds like a good idea. And don't forget, I could have married an ugly old bat if I was worried about people looking at my wife!'

She laughed. 'And I could have married a computer geek who collected anoraks!'

I grabbed her around the waist and pulled her towards me.

'With a body like yours it's definitely time we went to bed. Come on.'

We had chosen a room overlooking the River Arrin as our bedroom. It commanded magnificent views of the glen and the surrounding mountains. The river was close enough, when the window was open, to hear it pounding over the rocks as it flowed along the course of the valley towards the estuary mouth on the east coast. Late as it was, we made love with passionate energy fuelled by the lingering anticipation aroused by the atmosphere in the nightclub. It wasn't until dawn broke over the eastern peaks that we finally curled up and cuddled, spent in one another's arms.

We were enjoying a late breakfast in the kitchen when the telephone rang.

'I hope to goodness I haven't got to go off somewhere,' I said, bleary from our late night. 'I'm not expecting anyone today.'

I picked it up. 'Hallo.'

It was Sophie's mother.

'How are you?' I asked.

'We're fine,' she replied, somewhat curtly. 'But I'm afraid we've had some dreadful news. Can I talk to Sophie please?'

Leaving me completely in the dark, I passed the phone over.

'It's your mother,' I said bluntly. 'Something's happened.'

'Hi, Mum, what is it? Is Dad all right?'

I waited and watched Sophie's expression change from alarm to one of disbelieving shock. Apart from a few disjointed words I was unable to make any sense out of the conversation. It seemed like hours before she put the phone down and sat numbed, silent at the table.

'What's happened?' I asked, trying not to panic.

'I can't believe it,' she mumbled, 'it's Uncle William.'

'What about him?'

'He's dead.'

'Dead,' I cried in disbelief. 'Dead. But he can't be. We only spoke to him last week. What happened?'

'He died last night. Mrs Painter found him this morning. Rang Dad who's gone over there. I can't believe this.'

I felt numb. Uncle William had become a familiar constant in the short time that Sophie and I had been together. He had always been so supportive of us. He and Sophie, his niece and surrogate daughter, had been very close, talking at least once a week. It was a bitter shock.

Sophie started to cry. I tried to comfort her, hugging her reassuringly. She just sat there sobbing gently, drowning in the sorrows that no living being could alleviate.

'I need,' she whispered after a while, 'to go for a walk.'

'Come on,' I took her hand.

'No, on my own. You don't mind do you? I'll be all right. I just need some time.'

I was disappointed that she felt I couldn't help her but I realised that she had to grieve in her own way.

'Of course not,' I reassured her. 'I'll be here if you want me. Be careful.'

She stumbled miserably from the room and like an automaton fetched a coat.

'No, Bramble, not now. Just me. 'The dog looked dejected and sat down again by the Aga.

Despite my own shock I worried about Sophie. I didn't really like her going off in that state. I was wondering whether to follow her when the telephone rang again.

It was Sophie's father.

'I gather you've heard the awful news,' he said. 'I'm over at William's now.'

'Yes, Deirdre rang about half an hour ago. It's a terrible shock.'

'Is Sophie there?' he asked, 'I'd like a word with her.'

'No, she's gone for a walk. She needed some time alone I think. She's devastated.'

'Poor girl,' her father said. 'She's likely to take this harder than anyone I'm afraid. She was William's favourite, you know. They've always been incredibly close.'

'I'll get her to ring when she gets back. Do you know what happened?'

'Well, not yet. It seems as though he went to sleep in his armchair by the fire last night and never woke up. Probably a heart attack, the doctor said. Sad though, he was only fifty-five and seemed as fit as a fiddle.'

A wonderful way to go for him, I suppose, but somehow worse for those left behind. Such a shock. No warning.'

'Look after Sophie, James, she's going to need you. It may be a good idea if she comes home for a while. See what she wants after a day or two.'

'Yes, I will. And I'll get her to ring you when she gets back.'

I spent a lonely, anxious hour or so waiting for Sophie to return. I didn't feel like doing anything which made the time drag even more. Bramble lay contentedly by the Aga oblivious to the tragedy and I wished for a moment that I was a dog, untroubled by emotions or relationships. If Bramble's uncle died she was hardly likely to be on the phone ringing her mother.

Sophie eventually came back, her eyes red and swollen. She hugged me tightly, not saying a word.

'Come and sit down,' I suggested, pulling out a chair for her. 'You need a strong cup of tea.'

'I'm sorry I went off,' she said, trying to hold back the tears.

'Don't be,' I assured her, 'grief is a very personal thing. You have to deal with it in the way you think best.' I paused to fill up the teapot. 'Just as long as you know I'm with you.'

'I do know,' she replied. 'Thank you.'

She sipped the tea and sat quietly at the kitchen table.

'Your father wants you to ring him. He's at Cordwainers Hall now.'

'Oh, right, did he say if it was about anything special?'

'No, I guess he just wants to speak to you.'

We had an awful day not really sure of what to do and trying to take in the fact that Uncle William was dead.

There would be a lot of things for Sophie's father to sort out. He was the executor of the will. Various relatives telephoned during the day to talk to Sophie. Although I was deeply saddened by the sudden death of her uncle, I did not have the same closeness to him and my concern was for Sophie. She hardly said much at all. It was difficult to get her to eat.

When we finally went to bed that evening she seemed more devastated than ever.

'There's something I just can't get out of my mind,' she said, lying next to me wide awake.

'What's that?' I asked her gently.

'I keep thinking that while we were out enjoying ourselves last night, poor William was all alone dying.'

It was a sobering and true fact. I let it sink in before answering.

'Sophie, that's true. But it's not as though we knew or could have done anything, is it? It must be the same for millions of people all over the world.'

'I know, I know,' she said. 'I don't mean it in a morbid way, I just can't help thinking about it. Do you see what I mean?'

'Yes, of course I do. But it's better not to think of it like that. Remember how happy he seemed when we last saw him. That's a more helpful thought isn't it?'

Eventually we drifted off to sleep and despite Sophie's anguish, the emotionally draining effect of the day helped her sleep soundly. Mentally she was exhausted.

She decided not to go home straight away as the funeral was to be held the following Friday. Instead, we would stay down for that weekend.

The distraction of work in the estate office was good for me but Sophie had less to do. She spent a good part of each day riding Grehan around the estate getting to know the area. At least the weather was fine and even in her sorrow she found the beauty of the Highlands soothing.

Things weren't quite so calm in the office. On the Tuesday I had arranged for some aerial spraying to be carried out by helicopter on some of the lower slopes of the hill where bracken was encroaching on the heather and grasses. Bracken had no value to the deer or sheep which grazed the area. We had posted warning notices at the access points to the hill but this hadn't deterred a young German couple. Unseen by the pilot, the Germans, lying semi-naked in the bracken, had received a good soaking of Asulox. The chemical formulated to suppress growth had evidently suppressed someone's ardour and they arrived hot foot in the office.

Mrs McIver came rushing in. 'Och, Mr Aden,' she said, 'there's a wee storm brewing just now out 'ere. I've a young couple o' foreign people and I canna understan' a word they're sayin'.'

I went out into the hall. 'Hallo,' I said. 'How can I help?'

Their English left something to be desired and was harder to understand because of the heavy guttural intonation.

'Ve 'ave bin attacked from ze air,' the more masculine looking one told me.

I felt like saying that there was nothing new there then, and look where it got you before. However, bearing in mind that the estate belonged to Lord Rumshott and that his sister was a princess of a minor European principality, I answered with more diplomacy.

'Oh, dear,' I said, 'Where were you when this happened?'

The less masculine looking one said something in German and blushed nervously.

'Ve vere valking in ze hill. Just ere by ze river,' and she pointed towards the place in question.

'Ah, I see,' I replied. 'Well, you shouldn't have been there. There are warning signs explaining that we are spraying today. I'm sorry How come the pilot didn't see you?'

The couple conversed in German before the man replied, 'Ve vas having a rest in ze green plants.'

'That I'm afraid is what we were spraying.'

'This ist not gud. Vat are ve to do now? This stuff ist on us.'

'Well I doubt there's much to worry about. Where are you staying? Perhaps you could go back and have a shower.'

'Ve are camping in ze valley.'

'Oh. Well, I should have a swim in the river if you're worried,' I suggested.

The chances that much spray had got on to their skin seemed pretty slim and if they'd bothered to read our signs then it wouldn't have happened. 'The river's not cold.'

'Ve think you are unhelpful. Ve vill make a complaint.'

I didn't see what I could do and besides, it wasn't the best week I'd ever had, so I shrugged my shoulders and apologised again. The Germans seemed to realise that the meeting was over and with bad grace they departed.

'Ye ken ne'er tell what'll 'appen next here,' Mrs McIver informed me. 'Only last year we 'ad a bird-watcher fall off a cliff to 'is death. He was one o' them Germans too, you ken. Seem to tek a delight in getting into a mess.'

'Well, at least nobody died this time,' I said. 'Are there any other messages?'

'Aye, there's a message from Lord Rumshott. He and the viscountess are hoping to come up in two weeks' time to look at t'lodge. I gather there's a fair bit o' work they want done up there.'

'There is indeed,' I agreed. 'I'm not sure what it is but I understand that Lady Rumshott has ideas.'

In my experience when a ladyship had ideas we were in for a period of turmoil so I hoped that this younger ladyship hadn't caught anything nasty from her elders.

I thought that it would be useful to take a look around the lodge so that I would have a few ideas of my own. It was an impressive house built in the late 1800s on the edge of Loch Arrin overlooking the strath. To my mind it probably had one of the greatest views of anywhere in the Highlands. Set outside the village the long driveway, rough with stone shingle, led through thick masses of rhododendrons which hid the house from sight until the final bend. Suddenly there it was, with the loch and a stunning open expanse of the glen in full view, stretching as far as the eye could see. From that point, the estate stretched to the horizon in every direction. The mighty Glen Arrin estate encompassed 73,000 acres of breathtaking country.

The lodge had been built in the Victorian era when it had become fashionable for wealthy Englishmen to possess such status symbols. Glen Arrin had become a renowned deer forest and stalking was still its primary concern. The house, designed to accommodate large parties and the necessary staff, hadn't altered much since then and I believed that the Rumshotts were keen to try and make it a little less austere. It did have a somewhat stilted, grandiose air about it which was nowadays unfashionable. No doubt the enormous public rooms, billiards room and ballroom would remain unaltered but I suspected that the numerous service rooms, kitchens and pantries would be the target of the viscountess' attention.

The place was shut up and empty, with shutters closed and dust sheets covering many of the contents. I took the liberty of strolling through every room imagining past generations of formal guests being entertained in traditional Highland style. I spent a good couple of hours lost in my own reverie, blanking out the pressing heeds of the current world. But my thoughts kept returning to Uncle William, whose privileged life at his manor house in Suffolk was comparable, if on a smaller scale, to life in days gone by at the lodge.

At length I returned home to the manse and found Sophie, still sombre but in a much better mood. The ride around the tracks in the forest had refreshed some of her vitality and she was philosophical about the events that had unfolded without warning.

We telephoned her parents and made arrangements to travel down to England on the Thursday, intending to stay for a few days after the funeral.

Chapter 5

It was just as well we stayed for the extended weekend because another shock was to change the course of our lives for ever.

William Cavendish's funeral took place on the Friday afternoon as arranged and turned out to be a suitably respectful and, at the same time thankful, service commemorating his full and successful life. A large number of the mourners gathered afterwards for tea at Cordwainers Hall and it was evident that he had been a well-liked and popular figure. By six o'clock the house had emptied, leaving only the family, Mrs Painter and a stern-looking man who I had not noticed before. I guessed he was the family's solicitor as he wore a very formal black suit and there was a seriousness about him that only lawyers seem to possess.

'We'll go through to the dining room,' announced Sophie's father, 'as, there are various matters that we need to discuss.'

The assembled crowd followed him through. There was quite a number of us: Mr and Mrs Cavendish, Sophie and myself, Sophie's brother Harry once more returned from Australia, Mrs Painter and the solicitor who was introduced as Albert Wissington.

'I don't know as I should rightly be 'ere,' said Mrs Painter to Sophie's father. 'This be a family matter, not for the likes of me.'

'No,' he replied, 'I think you should be present; as the outcome of all this is going to affect you as much as anyone. You have, after all, been my brother's housekeeper for twenty years or more. You're almost a part of the family.'

We took our seats around the massive Georgian table, which was for once free of dust The silver pheasants standing in the centre were faintly distracting as it appeared that one was trying to mount the other. Mrs Painter had obviously thrown them together in a hurry.

'It is of course a dreadful day for all of us,' started Henry Cavendish gravely, 'and we will all miss William terribly I know.' He rested his gaze on Sophie longer than the rest of us. 'It is however the only chance that we have of being together in the immediate future and besides, there are matters that have to be dealt with swiftly.'

He paused. The manner in which Mr Wissington made his movements suggested that he was anxious to get down to business. The rest of us waited silently.

'I have asked Albert to read William's will but before he does so I want to explain that I am also an executor and am fully aware of its contents. In particular I mention this to Harry. William and I, together with Albert, jointly decided that this was the right decision to make.'

Harry looked as though he hadn't a clue what his father was talking about, and I suppose neither had we.

He continued, 'So Albert, I would be grateful if you would now read my brother William's last and final testament.'

Mr Wissington stood up and opened the papers lying in front of him on the table. From the inside pocket of his jacket he slowly withdrew a pair of half-moon spectacles, and with a practised dramatic flourish, placed them on his nose.

'I have here the last testament of William Henry Richard

Cavendish, resident of Cordwainers Hall, Suffolk, and it is my duty to disclose the contents to the assembled gathering.' He was enjoying the moment of ritual and the effect it was having on the group. Mrs Painter in particular, looked as though the world was coming to an end. She sat rigid in her seat, clinging to every word that was said. She was not, I am sure, expecting anything personally from the estate, but the formality was causing her some anguish.

The lawyer read out some small bequests made to a number of friends and charities.

'And to continue,' said Mr Wissington, 'I leave £20,000 to my long-serving, long-suffering housekeeper, Mrs Iris Painter.'

At this point there was a gasp and she stood up abruptly, jolting the happy pheasants. The cock fell over.

'My dear Lord,' she exclaimed, 'my goodness me. I don't know what to say.' She tottered for a minute before collapsing back on to her chair. 'Gawd bless 'is soul.'

'I'm sure He will,' went on Mr Wissington. 'And I know that he valued all you did for him over such a long period of time.'

There was some more paper shuffling before he cleared his throat and continued.

'And so to the remainder, which I add, is in effect almost all of William Cavendish's sizeable estate. I hereby leave Cordwainers Hall, together with its farm of 300 acres, the contents of the house and the residue of all my other assets, to my niece, Sophie Aden, née Cavendish.'

There was a long silence. Sophie looked shocked. She was shaking.

'I had no idea,' she said at last. 'Why on earth would he leave it all to me?'

She stared at her father.

'Because William and I decided that you, being the closest to him, should have Cordwainers and that Harry will eventually inherit the farm at home. It was always going to be the fairest way. We just didn't expect it to happen so devastatingly soon.'

With nothing seeming real, the meeting drew to a close. Mr Wissington departed to await instructions as to what would happen to the farm and Mrs Painter was charged with keeping the house running until a decision was made about its future. Everything was very uncertain and unsettling.

The Cavendishs and I returned to their home. The trip back to the house gave Sophie and I a chance to talk. Both of us were experiencing a kind of shocked disbelief.

'I can't take it in,' she said to me. 'It's going to change everything, isn't it?'

'I suppose so,' I answered. 'It depends on what you want to do. There are several options.'

'Do you mean sell the place?' she asked, horrified.

'Not necessarily. You could I suppose, though I doubt that is what you want. Or you could let it, or perhaps we could live there.'

She gazed out of the window silently.

'Would you want to live there?' she asked. 'It'd mean giving up Scotland, all the things you've worked towards. I mean we both planned this move up north. It was what we wanted to do together.'

'I know'

The predicament mulled around in my mind as we drove on. Whatever we decided it wasn't going to be easy. There were pluses and minuses on both sides and we would have to talk it through with Sophie's parents.

We left it to the following day but as her father pointed out, some decisions had to be made quickly.

Understandably her family was vehemently against selling the farm and it came down to whether to let it or go and live there.

'I'd have to find another job over there,' I remarked, 'but I'm not against the idea. We couldn't after all live off 300 acres in today's farming climate.'

Mr Cavendish agreed. 'Mind you,' he added, 'William's estate also includes a reasonable income from his other assets, share portfolio and that sort of thing. You need to have another meeting with Wissington to discuss all that and I'm afraid all the inheritance tax implications. There's an awful lot to be sorted out.'

'What's your gut feeling, Sophie?'

'I have to say,' she said slowly, 'that my gut feeling is that we should move there. Make it our home, farm it as Uncle William would have wanted. I think I'd feel restless up in Scotland, anywhere come to that, knowing Cordwainers Hall was there and it was now mine, or ours rather. I absolutely adore the place.'

The next few days were spent in a state of indecision. We had a hugely important decision to make, one that would undoubtedly change our lives. It was clearly the first test of our marriage. We discussed it at length with Sophie's parents, had a further meeting with the solicitor, who told us that we would never be poor, and spent a day at Cordwainers Hall.

It was the day we spent by ourselves at the hall that made up our minds. A glorious sunny day with the farm basking in the splendour of early summer and the gardens a riot of scent and colour made us realise that we had to grasp the opportunity. The faded grandeur of the house itself lent another exciting dimension. It was a beautiful, impressive manor house which with a lot of love and attention could be turned into something very special. The dilapidated air that William Cavendish had enjoyed was part of his eccentricity. But as a family home it could be magnificent.

There followed a period of intense activity. The Cavendishs were delighted, as was Mrs Painter who would stay on as our housekeeper. Mr Wissington also seemed pleased although his dour formal attitude permitted him only the merest smile of approval. The difficult part was leaving the Highlands. We had only just begun to settle in and it was with anguish that I met Viscount Rumshott to explain the changed circumstances.

Sophie came back to the manse for a fortnight and then left for Suffolk. I spent a sad month waiting for my replacement to arrive, acting more as a caretaker than instigating anything useful. I was going to miss the wonderful, beautiful remoteness of the Scottish Highlands and I felt desperately sorry that my chance to live amongst it all had been taken from me, albeit by a generous and exciting alternative. The only real blot on the horizon was that I would have to use motorway service stations on my way back to England.

Chapter 6

Our life at Cordwainers Hall began in a whirlwind. Sophie and Mrs Painter spent ages working on the house altering things around so that it didn't look exactly the same as when William Cavendish had been alive. We stored all our own furniture in the dining room but at some point a major sort out would have to be undertaken. Outside it was even busier. The sheep needed attention, the barley needed spraying and the gardens were in full growth. Fortunately there was some help. Apart from Mrs Painter, Mr Cavendish had also employed a general farmworker and a gardener, both of whom had cottages on the farm. Although a farm of this size could not afford such extravagances, it seemed as though the investment portfolio could.

The farm man, Bert Flat, had been born on the farm sixty years earlier, but looked about 120 years older. He had the Grand Canyon of crags on a weather-beaten face and was so stooped that it was impossible to meet his eye unless he was sitting down or 1 was crouched on the ground. But appearances were misleading. He worked tirelessly and made me feel as though I was chronically lazy. The gardener was his identical twin brother Reginald and inside it was almost impossible to tell them apart. One had more chance outside because they wore different hats, Bert favouring a flat cap while Reg usually sported a deerstalker. Both men were unmarried and lived in adjoining cottages and, according to Mrs Painter, only visited each other's house on Christmas Day. Of course their paths would cross regularly during the working day but the merest of grunts was the sole mark of recognition.

Sophie and I quickly settled into the routine of having a farm to run. It seemed strange as when we had left Harbottle just three months earlier I had expected that to be the end of our farming careers. To be so soon back into the fray was a surprise but a welcome one as we loved it, realising in retrospect how much we had missed the life. We even had a few old friends back, Jess the collie and some of the young ewes I had bred. We had been fortunate that William Cavendish had taken them on when we had moved to Scotland.

Although we relished the life and the fact that we could spend our time together jointly working on a future, we were aware that the farm would not be able to support so many people. Apart from ourselves, the Flat brothers and Mrs Painter had to be paid and we didn't want to change any of Uncle William's arrangements. The other income left to us helped of course, but some of that we needed to spend on the hall and it appeared unlikely that it would be sufficient over the long term.

We decided on a plan of action. The farm would stay as it was and Sophie would manage it, carrying out all the office work and helping physically when she could. I would look for a job locally, probably accepting a post in a firm rather than as agent on an estate. As I had spent five years training to become a chartered surveyor in order to manage landed estates and I had worked for Lord Leghorn and Viscount Rumshott I was confident that it would not be long before I found a suitable position. It was therefore with enthusiasm that I began my search, endlessly sending off CVs to all and sundry. However, as the weeks went by I began to have doubts. People would write kind letters, thanking me for my application and assuring me of my suitability but all their positions were spoken for. I began to question if I had done the right thing by leaving Scotland so swiftly. Perhaps I should have carried on up there until I had found a position in Suffolk. Perhaps I could have left Sophie to look after Cordwainers until I was ready to join her. The one slight consolation was that I had been offered a number of jobs as an estate agent selling houses but such a post would have been a waste of my training and experience. Besides, I had no desire to spend my days measuring room sizes and inventing complimentary descriptions of people's houses. Fortunately there was enough money in the bank to allow me to carry on the pursuit of a job in the career I really wanted. Nonetheless it was a very demoralising search and I was beginning to think that estate agency might be the only option when a chance encounter in the local pub went a long way to assuring my future.

Cordwainers Hall was an isolated house set in a hollow of the rolling Suffolk countryside. It had no immediate neighbours unless one counted the dead ones lying in the graveyard of the adjoining church. A long drive separated the house from the hamlet of Cordwainers and the farm buildings were reached via a different back drive nearer the hamlet. Cordwainers itself was a quiet place and the only excitement of any note was the post box. As a consequence any social activities centred on the closest village two miles away Frampton.

Frampton had nearly everything one could want. It was an extraordinarily attractive place, with genuine Tudor houses aplenty. A sensitive conservation policy had ensured that no pale imitations of the real thing were allowed in the village. The jewel of Frampton's crown was its famous market square, which attracted thousands of tourists each year. The tourists kept the local economy afloat, supporting a wide variety of shops and a similarly diverse selection of restaurants and pubs. It formed the centre of a large estate owned by the Buckley family who, in landowning terms, were neighbours of ours at Cordwainers. But we were hardly on an even footing as they were our neighbours on three sides. I had enquired whether there might be a job suitable for me on the estate but the agent had assured me that he was there to stay.

Sophie and I had gone over to Frampton one Saturday evening for a pub meal in The Anne of Cleves and were sitting at the bar afterwards chatting when a portly gentleman wandered in, accompanied by a rabbit on a lead.

We assumed that he was a regular as no one seemed surprised. He stood next to us drinking a pint of Guinness and all would have been well except that a dog, sitting under a nearby table, took an interest in the rabbit and launched itself across the room. In the ensuing fracas Sophie ended up drenched in Guinness. The rabbit man, extremely upset and embarrassed by the mishap, insisted on buying us a round of drinks and we got into conversation with him.

He was, he told us, an upholsterer who lived in the village, and had always kept a pet rabbit ever since he was a boy. I didn't ask why he took it around with him like a dog. It was more interesting for the rabbit I suppose, than being kept in a wooden box with a carrot for company. During a lull in the conversation – after all, there is only so much one can say to an upholsterer with a rabbit – the landlord butted in.

''Tis a strange do up at the Hall, isn't it, Fred?'

'Eh?'

'Said it's a funny old business with Mr Bridges. You 'ave 'eard, I suppose?' the landlord repeated.

'Heard what, Alan?'

''Bout Mr Bridges leaving. He went yesterday. Cleared orf, just like that. Poor Sir Charles is in a right state about it by all accounts.'

Sophie started talking to me about something else but I interrupted her.

'Ssh, sorry, darling, but did you overhear what they're saying? I think Bridges was the name of the agent here.'

The barman was expanding on the details.

'Yeah, he's done a runner with whatsername up at Cow Parsley Farm.'

'Has he?' the upholsterer replied. 'Do you know, I've just restuffed a Chesterfield for 'em.'

'You mean the Galworthys, don't you?'

'That's the name, Galworthy.'

'I wouldn't have thought Mrs had it in her to do . . .'

'It weren't the wife, it were the daughter he's taken.'

'The daughter!' Fred exclaimed in surprise. 'Well I didn't think she were very old but I could be mistaken.'

'She isn't. She's sixteen or seventeen, I should say 'bout half Bridges' age. But she was, how can I put it, experienced when it came to men. A head turner too. You could see all the blokes in here gawping at her tidy little arse whenever she walked in.'

'Lucky old Bridges.' He chuckled. 'That'll keep 'im lively. Where 'ave they gone d'you know?'

The landlord turned to serve another customer before continuing.

'Don't know as yet,' he said, 'but neither her parents or Sir Charles are very happy about it, as you can imagine. There's even talk 'bout her being pregnant, but I don't know whether that's true. And you know me, I never like to gossip.'

I heard Sophie stifle a giggle. I decided to risk interrupting them.

'Excuse me but isn't Mr Bridges Sir Charles Buckley's agent?' I asked.

'Oh, you know him, do you?' enquired the landlord. 'I didn't think you was a local.'

'Well, we're not really,' I explained. 'We've recently moved to Cordwainers and I thought I recognised the name.'

'Oh, I see. You must be poor old Mr Cavendish's family then? I heard his niece or some such had taken over up there.'

'Sophie's his niece,' I explained.

'There's always summat seems to be changing about 'ere,' he continued, 'like this to-do with Bridges. He was the agent here, and a pretty good one I'd say. It'll put the estate in a right muddle for a while I've no doubt.'

I looked at Sophie who laughed mischievously.

'We'd better go home and get writing!' she suggested. 'Could be just the break you need. Mind you, I hope it's not catching – I don't want you having any ideas of running off with a teenage nymphet!'

I grabbed her around the waist and kissed the warm soft nape of her neck hidden under her long dark hair.

'You,' I assured her, 'need have no fear of that. You're the sexiest, most adorable nymphet there is! Come on, I'll race you to the car.'

I wrote to Sir Charles Buckley that evening explaining my circumstances and how we had come to inherit the farm at Cordwainers. Two days later he telephoned and asked me to go and see him. We met in the estate office in the market place at Frampton. The interview lasted for about five minutes, during which he checked whether I liked dogs, rode horses and could shoot. He had known William Cavendish and was a friend of Lord Leghorn and on that basis gave me the job. The finer details, he said, would be sorted out by the estate lawyer and he asked the office secretary to give me Gordon White's telephone number.

When I returned home, I was a little unsure as to whether I had really got the job or not.

'How did it go?' Sophie asked.

'Well, I think I got it,' I replied hesitantly.

'What do you mean think? Were you offered it?'

'Sort of,' I explained. 'He asked me if I liked dogs and that was about it. I've got to ring his lawyer to sort out the details. I don't know any more than that.'

In due course I met the lawyer and fortunately, in complete contrast to Sir Charles, we had a long and detailed discussion about the estate, the family and the job. Although the daily contact was very much to be with the baronet, almost all the planning and financial administration was in communication with the solicitors. It became a little more obvious why Sir Charles had left the crux of the interview to Gordon White.

He asked me to start in a fortnight's time, giving him the chance to follow up my references. He offered me a reasonable salary and an understanding that I would be able to continue my involvement with the farm as an aside to my job.

After the turmoil over the past few months we felt a huge relief that our lives could settle down. Whatever other changes might happen we would stay at Cordwainers and hopefully I would enjoy my career as agent at Frampton. There was of course a lot to do at the farm, both with the business and the house. But that was now our passion and one that would last for years.

Chapter 7

For the first several weeks my new life in Sir Charles' estate office went smoothly enough. But by now I was experienced enough as a land agent to know that it was likely to be the lull before the storm. At Rumshott lost parrots and fugitive sheep had often been on the day's agenda and while so far my time at the Frampton estate had been spent dealing with matters that clearly did fall within my job description I refused to believe that this was going to last. The day had now come. Sir Charles had managed to run over Miss Smithson's handbag.

Fortunately it wasn't attached to her arm at the time and to be fair Sir Charles did not notice anything even though the weight of the car had set off her rape alarm. He continued driving down the village's main street leaving the alarm screeching in the roadway, and a little later, Miss Smithson came screeching into the estate office. She had in her youth apparently been much feted by the young men of the locality and it remained a mystery as to why she had never married. It wasn't likely to happen now as she was well into her nineties. Although frail it swiftly became apparent that her vocal chords were still in good health. She tottered into the office, a walking stick in one hand and a scuffed piece of black leather in the other.

'Mr Aden please,' she demanded in a voice so loud I could heard her clearly from my office.

'I'll see if he's in for you, Miss Smithson,' said Anne, the estate secretary, getting up from behind her desk.

'Yes, show her in,' I answered to the knock on my office door as Anne's face appeared.

I greeted Miss Smithson and helped her to a chair, pushing aside various files, estate maps and a stuffed monkey that had arrived mysteriously in the office the previous week, addressed to Sir Charles' son, Sebastian.

'Sir Charles has run over my handbag,' she quavered, depositing the thing on my desk. 'Take a look, Mr Aden, everything is ruined.'

The theory that men can never understand the logic behind the contents of a lady's handbag was confirmed as I gingerly picked through its contents. Ironically the one item that she probably needed most had caused the trouble. I carefully picked out the blue glass fragments of a broken bottle of milk of magnesium. The medicine had seeped through her papers like unset glue.

'Are you sure you want me to go through all your private things here, Miss Smithson?' I asked, a little wary of discovering something untoward.

'You must,' she cried plaintively. 'I expect the estate to put good the damage Sir Charles has caused.'

I refrained from pointing out that if she hadn't left her handbag in the road then this would never have happened. She was after all one of the estate's oldest tenants and as such it was our place to help, whatever the cause of her distress. I was rather surprised to find a driving licence and a passport. Miss Smithson could not drive a car and had never travelled more than ten miles from Frampton, let alone crossed the sea.

'Well, some of these things aren't really important,' I commented, 'but anything that's damaged we will get replaced.'

'What do you mean, not important?' she queried.

'Um, well the passport and driving licence immediately spring to mind. You don't use either of them, do you?'

She looked at me aghast and I couldn't help noticing that the expression on her face was beginning to resemble the one on the stuffed monkey sitting beside her.

'But I like to have them in case of an emergency,' she explained.

'Oh, I see,' I said, not really seeing what kind of emergency would be assisted by Miss Smithson's ability to drive a car or jump on a plane.

'But in any case they have both expired,' I continued, wiping milk of magnesium off the pages. 'So I don't think we can do much about those. However, I'm sure Sir Charles would be only too happy to pay for some new spectacles,' I said, holding up a pair of pince-nez with no glass in them.

They seemed to be covered in congealed blood but upon delving further into the depths of the handbag I found a broken tube of bright red lipstick.

'I'll make a list of everything that's broken and get Anne to take you to town and buy some replacements. I think that would be the best way of sorting this out don't you?'

'Yes, I think so too,' she agreed, 'but I do want my documents back before I leave.'

I rang through to Anne on the office telephone.

'Could you take Miss Smithson into town and do some shopping for her,' I asked, explaining the situation.

'Of course, I'll come through and see her,' she said.

'Right, Miss Smithson. I shall let Sir Charles know what's happened but I'm afraid I've got to leave you with Anne now as I'm due up at the Hall.'

Anne was an eminently capable woman who had run the estate office for fifteen years and was used to dealing with the most unusual of problems. The office's location in the square meant that we were easy prey for villagers with too much time on their hands. It often seemed as though they were coming in for a bit of company, rather than to draw attention to some aspect of the running of the estate. Personally I would have preferred the office to be up at the Hall, a mile out of the village, but Sir Charles had a vaguely philanthropic view that he wanted it to be convenient for his tenants.

My new employer Sir Charles Buckley, KG, DSO, eighth baronet, was an unusually thin man. Aged in his early seventies, six feet two tall, white hair and a precisely trimmed handlebar moustache, I'd once overheard one of the tenant farmers remark that he'd 'seen more meat on a sparrow's kneecap'. Sir Charles was also extremely rich, and like many wealthy men, extremely frugal with it. Amongst other assets he owned the 10,000 acres of Frampton Hall Estate, property in London, Scotland and Canada, and an art collection generally held to be one of the finest in private hands in the world. Although his clothes were tailored from the finest quality cloth he had been wearing them for nearly half a century. From a distance one might think that he was the gardener on a particularly unkempt day. He held the view that it didn't matter how he dressed in the country as everyone knew him. And it didn't matter how he dressed in town as nobody knew him.

Sir Charles was a widower and lived on his own in Frampton Hall. The house was massive, a huge Palladian-fronted mansion set in 300 acres of parkland. Behind the Palladian front the building spread out in a muddle of architectural styles. A red-brick Tudor wing was largely unused, having been superseded by a later Gothic monstrosity along the east front. No one had ever bothered to count exactly how many rooms there were. It covered such a vast area that in the early 1900s a man had been employed full time simply to wind all the clocks in the house. There was a warren of corridors and passages, thirty staircases, an estimated three miles of heating pipes, nine acres of carpets and two telephones.

When it came to spending money Sir Charles veered between the careful and the spendthrift. He considered telephones a luxury and the near absence of them in a house the size of a small town made it notoriously difficult to get hold of him. Conversely, he felt a reasonably sized staff was necessary and he employed a butler, two footmen, a cook, a housekeeper and eight full-time maids. A head gardener, two under gardeners and three grooms completed his household staff.

My job was similar to the ones at Rumshott and Glen Arrin, overseeing the running of the estate, the staff and the tenants. Apart from Anne, the secretary, the estate office also employed an accounts clerk and a farm secretary. They all lived in estate cottages in the village, a tightly knit community whose defining characteristic was its inhabitants' seemingly insatiable lust for gossip. Anne, a solid character of a woman, took everything in her stride and nothing ever seemed to surprise her. A very capable secretary, she considered gossip to be beneath her, but then so did most of the village.

Brenda, the accounts clerk, was so quiet and timid it was easy to forget that she was there. She simply got on with her work in a rather boring sort of way and provided the rest of us with no excitement whatsoever. I often wondered why Sir Charles had employed her because although she was efficient her taciturnity did not inspire much confidence. The mystery was perhaps explained by her resemblance to some of Sir Charles' favourite pets, his standard poodles, although he referred to them as water retrievers. Like Sir Charles' breed, Brenda had the distinction of tight curly black hair and a long nose which tapered into a snout.

The other person in the office, Gail Hartson, the farm secretary, was a buxom blonde divorcee with two teenage daughters. Having divorced, Gail was clearly minded to embrace the politics of sexual liberation. While she may have thought this was what she was doing, to others it seemed as though she had regressed to her sixteen-year-old self, when she had experimented with several men in an effort to find the right partner. If she had been more discreet about her male friends she might have saved herself much embarrassment although life in the office would have been rather less exciting.

It was at Gail's behest that I was due up at the Hall to see Sir Charles. As the farm secretary she had been approached by a producers' group which promoted and sold locally made specialist foods. On their behalf Gail had asked Sir Charles to host a farmers' market in the square and now I was expected to organise the event.

I drove the mile or so up to the Hall through the ancient parkland. The carriage drive approach across the rolling countryside offered visitors tantalising glimpses of the house, the magnificent lake, and the majestic stands of centuries-old oak trees before reaching an impressive lime avenue that stretched towards the south front of the Hall. I continued on to the east front which abutted the stable block and entered through the staff quarters.

'Ah, good morning, Mr Hole,' I shouted as I saw the butler disappearing at the end of the corridor.

He stopped. A man of few words and still fewer emotions he stared at me impassively.

'Is Sir Charles in his study, do you know?' I asked.

'I believe he is sir. Please, follow me.'

As I followed him through the labyrinth of corridors, I reflected how archaic it seemed, in a world of computers, internet and e-mail, that I was plodding along behind a butler dressed in a full livery tailcoat to find a man who relied on his staff, a fountain pen and his morning's copy of *The Times* to keep abreast of world events.

Having walked halfway back to the village we arrived at the study door. Hole knocked and opened it.

'Sir Charles, Mr Aden to see you,' he announced and showed me in.

Sir Charles was fast asleep in an armchair with a newspaper draped over him and his tray of coffee pot and biscuits balanced by his side. Hole, standing by the door, hadn't noticed so I quickly turned back towards him.

'He's fast asleep, Mr Hole,' I whispered, 'we'd better go out and try again. Knock a bit harder to wake him up, save any embarrassment.'

We crept out of the room and began the proceedings again. Hole knocked loudly on the door and waited. This time there was a muffled cry and then a sickening crash of breaking china. Hole's expression didn't falter.

'Oh, dear,' I said. 'I think he's knocked the table over.'

He stared at me impassively.

'I expect so, Mr Aden,' he replied, before opening the door for the second time.

'Good morning, Sir Charles,' I said, walking into the room with some degree of apprehension. The baronet, together with his newspaper, coffee tray and biscuits were all on the floor. He looked up.

'Morning, James. Knocked the bloody pot orf the tray,'

he explained unnecessarily. 'Hole gave me a bit of a start there.'

One of his poodles was devouring the biscuits with great enthusiasm whilst Sir Charles was hesitantly poking about with bits of broken china.

'Hole,' he continued, 'do you think you could get Mrs Jubb to come and sort out this mess please? Better bring a fresh lot through as well.'

'Very good, Sir Charles,' and Hole departed on his long walk back to the kitchens.

'Well we'd better get orn,' Sir Charles suggested as he went to sit down behind a huge eighteenth-century partner's desk. 'And come here, Napoleon . . . leave those damn biscuits alone.'

I settled down opposite him and placed a file on the desk.

'Now, what've we got today hmm?' he asked. 'Something about a fair in the square eh?'

'Yes sir. I briefly mentioned it the other day. As president of the Eastern Shires Fine Food Association you apparently offered to let them hold a farmers' market in the market place should they wish. Gail has had a request that they would like to do so.'

'Ah, yes, I remember. Jolly good idea this, you know, James. Promotes all these delicious foods being produced in the area. I order from several of them now. Quite remarkable what ideas they come up with.'

I recalled the last remarkable thing I'd eaten at a similar fair. It was some kind of sheep's milk cheese with an unpronounceable name. Tasting like a pencil eraser it had even squeaked alarmingly as I chewed.

'Yes, they do have some unusual products,' I agreed. 'Anyway they'd like to hold this on 20 July and obviously hope that you can attend.'

Sir Charles leafed through his diary.

'Absolutely fine,' he said. 'I'll look forward to it. I'll leave you to organise it.'

'Very good, sir. I think Gail Hartson would like to be involved. After all, the initial approach was made to her.'

'Fine, fine. By the way is she any more settled now?'

He was referring to Gail's insatiable appetite for men, each affair providing great entertainment for the village and tears in the estate office as she was consoled by whichever member of staff happened to be in at the time.

'I hope so, Sir Charles. She seems to be in a bit of a lull at the moment. I think the problem with the fish and chip shop man has put her off a bit.'

'I never really fathomed out what happened there,' he said, 'apart from what I read in the local papers.'

'I'm afraid she bit off more than she could chew. When the man's wife found out what was going on she set fire to his van. Dropped a match into the chip oil by all accounts. Left the chap with no business and nowhere to live.'

'She's a bit unlucky with her suitors, I always think,' he mused. 'Still I'm sure something will turn up sooner or later.'

'Well, it would give us some peace if it did,' I reflected. 'Whilst I remember, Sir Charles, apparently you ran over Miss Smithson's handbag earlier this morning. She'd dropped it in the road.'

He looked rather startled. 'Did I? Don't remember seeing it, or her come to that. Is it damaged?'

'I'm afraid so. Some of the contents were broken, her glasses, that sort of thing. I've asked Anne to sort out some replacements but I thought you might like to drop her a line.'

'Absolutely. How damned embarrassing. Can't think how I didn't notice.'

Knowing how little interest he took in either his car or his driving I could easily imagine how he hadn't noticed but refrained from saying so.

The replacement coffee arrived as I left and returned to the office. Thinking about Miss Smithson I remembered that I had forgotten about the stuffed monkey. Blast, I'd meant to ask him what it was doing in my office and what he wanted me to do with it. Presumably, Sebastian had left some instructions.

I met Gail in the office reception hall just as she was leaving for lunch.

'20 July is fine for the farmers' market,' I said.

'That's excellent. We can go ahead with the organisation then can we?'

'Yup, I'll need all the help you can give,' I replied.

I watched her heading in the direction of the bakers and supposed that some men might find her attractive. Although she wasn't my type at all even I could see that her manner of walking was designed to accentuate her somewhat full and curvaceous figure. I didn't know if she thought of herself as the Marilyn Monroe of Frampton but I wouldn't have been at all surprised.

Chapter 8

The weekend of the farmers' market was soon upon us. After several meetings with David Harold, the chairman of the producers' group, we had agreed how many stalls the market square could hold, what time the market would open and close, and after a little haggling, what price was to be exacted from the farmers. While Sir Charles was keen to help the farmers as much as possible there would inevitably be costs to the estate and so it was my job to make sure that these were covered, and if there was a little bit left over, well, so much the better. In the end we decided to make the hire of the stall space free but to ask for ten per cent of each stall's takings. That way if they made a profit the estate could share in that and if they did not we would not have exacerbated their problems.

Gail was left to make the individual arrangements with the stallholders. She decided what time they could start to put up their displays and she was judge and jury when it came to deciding which stall went where. Naturally, there was much negotiation over position and I think Gail rather enjoyed her position of power. I had simply suggested that she put the ones which she thought would be most popular in the most prominent positions.

All the stalls were taken three weeks before the event was due to take place. As long as the weather was good we were confident the day would be a success, for two reasons. Firstly, the standard of some of the stalls would be outstanding, with producers with reputations for top-quality organic meat and vegetables coming for the day. Secondly, Frampton ought to be full of people. It was the middle of the tourist season and the thousands who descended upon the village each week in the summer would be in the mood to part with their cash.

While most of the stalls were to be taken up by purveyors of fine foods the size of the square had enabled Gail to find space for some quirkier operators. Tucked away in the furthest corner of the square would be sellers of squirrel meat, life-enhancing crystals and various brands of New Age therapy. The stall had been let to the squirrel meat seller as a favour to Gail's father's second cousin while the other two were just fancies of Gail's. Heaven alone knew what you would be able to buy at the new age therapy stall. I did know, however, that it was unlikely that I would be parting with any cash there.

The other feature that would distinguish our market was the presence of a display of Suffolk Punches. We had had an approach from a rare breeds society asking if there was anything we could offer and Sir Charles had readily suggested we put them on show. There would be excellent publicity for the breed and hopefully plenty of money would be raised to help slow the decline in their numbers.

As I drew back the curtains on 20 July, I could see that we were to be blessed with fine weather. The market was to open at nine o'clock but I wanted to be there by six to smooth over any potential problems. I did not mind the early start as there was something magnificent about seeing the sun break through the darkness to provide the optimism of a new day. Looking out of our bedroom window the silence, interrupted only by the soft hum of Sophie's breathing, combined with the bold colours of the sky to make me feel truly humble. I kissed Sophie lightly on her forehead, grateful that I would be coming home to her later, and left the house as quietly as I could.

When I arrived at the square it was apparent that Gail had been there for some time. It was also obvious that the responsibility of helping to organise the market had gone to her head. Wearing a powder-pink suit and even more makeup than usual she may have been dressed appropriately for a business meeting in the City but in the context of a farmers' market, it was unusual to say the least. I could not resist the temptation to tease her.

'Hallo, Gail,' I said, 'that's a splendid outfit you've got on.'

'Thank you, James,' she replied, 'I bought it in town on Thursday night. It was ever so expensive.'

'Well, mind out for the horses when they arrive. There'll be plenty of muck about.'

With over thirty stalls setting up there was much to do. I checked the condition of the generator and its back-up. This would be a crucial day for the meat sellers and we did not want their refrigeration units powerless. It was also an opportunity to meet and greet the local farmers although Gail seemed to see this as her responsibility.

I went over to greet James Owen who would be selling his organically reared chickens. Since switching to organic production he had gained a reputation as the provider of the tastiest chickens in the whole of East Anglia. From struggling to keep the family farm going business was now booming. A ruddy-faced man, as thick of hair as he was of girth he always had some sort of scheme on the go.

'Morning, Mr Owen,' I said in my cheeriest possible voice.

'Morning, Mr Aden,' came the reply. 'I hope you've got

as many customers coming as you promised. I can't be lugging these chickens back and forth all the time. Ruins my cost analysis.'

'I haven't promised anything. But it should be a good day. There's been plenty of publicity and the sun should do the rest.'

'Well, I'll come and find you if I don't get what you've promised.'

When the market opened to the public business was initially slow, with only locals arriving in the square, but I soon cheered up as the longer the day wore on, the more people seemed to throng the square. Even the squirrel man seemed to be doing well. I noted with wry amusement that he had gone for the top end of the market and was marketing his produce as exotic although I didn't fancy eating bushy-tailed rodents, whatever description he used.

I saw Gail talking to one of the grooms looking after the Suffolk Punches and called out to her. The horses looked magnificent, their size and gait clear indicators of their power. I ruminated briefly about how sad it was that the progress in agricultural machinery was sending these proud animals headlong towards their extinction but I was interrupted from my reverie by the sight of Gail literally skipping over towards me, with a grin as wide as the Cheddar Gorge.

'Oh, James,' she yelped, 'isn't it going well?'

'Yes, and it looks as though the weather's going to hold. I imagine there'll be a tidy sum going into the estate's coffers,' I replied.

'We must make sure that Sir Charles lets us organise another one next year, or even sooner.'

'I'm sure he will. Certainly next year, anyway. That reminds me, he should be here soon.'

Sure enough Sir Charles arrived a few minutes later. I took him round the stalls introducing him to each vendor in turn. It felt as though I was showing the Queen around a hospital and it seemed that Sir Charles felt the same way. After a dialogue of inane comments regarding jam, bacon and sausages we concluded our tour.

'Well, James, it seems to have been a great success. I must say, I thought it would be,' Sir Charles commented.

'Yes, sir,' I replied. 'I think everyone's enjoyed it.'

'Well, all credit to you. And Gail, of course. That reminds me, I'd better congratulate her.'

'She'll be delighted to hear that. I'll go and find her for you, Sir Charles.'

I searched all over for Gail. The square was not that big but that was part of the problem. The teeming mass of people meant that whatever progress was made through the crowd was slow. If Gail was doing the same, there was little chance we would meet until the market's popularity abated.

I decided to give up and made my way back to Sir Charles to explain the situation. He didn't mind.

'Never mind, James,' he said, 'just remind me to telephone her on Monday morning.'

'Of course, sir,' I replied and that was the last I saw of Sir Charles that day. He had done his bit and now he wanted to return to the relative peace of his home.

As the afternoon turned towards evening the crowd in the square began to thin. Many of the stalls had sold out all of their produce and most of the rest did not have much left. I was slightly disturbed that there was still no sign of Gail but was sure she would turn up in the end. I decided to pay a visit to James Owen.

'Evening, Mr Owen, had a good day I hope.'

'I've sold every chicken I brought with me, Mr Aden,' he

responded. 'If you had told me how big it was going to be I would have bought more. So it seems to me that as you've cut into my profits with your poor information there should be some compensation.'

'That won't be possible, Mr Owen,' I said sternly, wondering if he would ever be grateful for anything.

'I know that,' he smiled. 'Just having a joke. Really, it's been a brilliant day. There'll be a pint on the table for you in the Anne of Cleyes.'

'That's very kind,' I replied, suddenly feeling thirsty.

'Nonsense. Think of it as a small thank-you for all your trouble.'

I smiled inwardly. If James Owen was prepared to buy me a pint then I really must be doing something right.

At last I saw Gail in the distance. I was grateful that this time she was walking towards me as I had found her skipping distracting.

'Gail, where have you been?' I asked. 'I've been looking all over for you. Sir Charles wanted to congratulate you on how well organised the day has been.'

'I am sorry, James,' she replied. I wasn't feeling very well so I went home for a bit. I would have told you but I couldn't find you in the crowds. I think the sun must have got to me.'

'Oh, well, not to worry,' I said, noticing bits of straw in her hair, 'as long as you're not ill, that's the main thing.'

When I eventually got home I relayed my suspicion of Gail and the groom to Sophie.

'Oh, dear, that'll mean more tears before bedtime, I suppose.'

'Well, I hope the relationship will last longer than that,' I replied, though I could hear the doubt in my voice as I spoke.

Chapter 9

Not long after the farmers' market, Sophie and I were invited to dinner by some senior partners of a national firm of land agents who wanted to take on the management contract of the estate woodlands. There were a thousand acres of woods, many of them in a neglected state, and I had suggested to Sir Charles that we did something about them.

I arranged to meet them at Le Champignon, a French restaurant of extraordinary quality which we were fortunate to have in the village. While the restaurant was owned by the Duponts I had some professional contact with them as they rented a house from Sir Charles to use as living quarters for some of their staff.

The importance of the instruction to Messrs Wright, Coke and Co. was evident as the local partner, Tony East, was joined by his boss from London, Horace Sullivan, and their respective wives. It was a rather odd and unnecessary evening and if it hadn't been held so close I doubt that I would have accepted the invitation, particularly as Sophie had already arranged to spend the evening with some old school friends and couldn't join us.

Tony East I knew slightly – a jolly rotund fellow with a large red face and huge bulging eyes. He looked as though he was being strangled but when he spoke, his voice soon put the lie to that idea. An auctioneer by training, his words boomed across the restaurant despite his constant reassurances that 'this discussion's just between us' and a lot of 'in confidence, I'll say this'. His wife, whose name I forgot, didn't utter a word all evening.

Mr Sullivan was different. A lean man with the air of an army officer, his conversation was direct and to the point. His wife, whose hobby was spinning wool so she told me, asked incessant questions about the history of Frampton and its origins as a medieval wool town.

'I think that the best way to proceed with any ideas is to have a trip around the woods to see what's there,' suggested Mr Sullivan, 'and preferably a meeting with Sir Charles.'

'That's fine,' I agreed, 'and I'll ring with some dates to fix a mutually convenient time.'

'What are the estate's main objectives regarding the commercial aspect of the woodlands?' asked Mr Sullivan.

'Well, firstly, we need to know what timber value there is,' I started before being interrupted by someone standing behind me saying, ''Ave you choosen se desires for se dinnere, please?'

I looked around. An absolutely stunning-looking girl stood there holding a menu. Very happily married to Sophie, it was only human to have noticed her.

'Er, I'll have the salade de chevre followed by the canard avec framboises, please,' I muttered.

Although I wasn't thrilled by my company for the evening the food was exceptional and I was entertained by the stunning waitress' attempts to make eye contact with me. Whenever I looked up she seemed to be smiling at me, provocatively running her hand through her hair. Deeply flattered, I smiled back, grateful that now I was happily married I wouldn't have to go through the agonies of the dating game again.

Sir Charles was very enthusiastic when I saw him to

discuss Messrs Wright, Coke and Co.'s involvement in the woodland management. Usually he dismissed such ideas with, 'You do whatever you think is best, James. I'll leave it to you.'

Part of this was no doubt due to his passion for trees. He had established a much regarded arboretum in the grounds of the Hall and was distressed by the condition of the estate woodlands.

'In my great grandfather's time,' he told me, 'the woods were immaculate you know. I remember as a small boy being taken through them in a pony and trap. The rides were kept mown, the trees pruned. Beautiful clean straight trunks. Not a weed anywhere unless it had been left for game cover.'

I had seen old photos and indeed what he said was true. The main difference now was that we had two woodmen on the staff while the fifth baronet had employed twenty.

'We'll have those chaps here for coffee beforehand, then take 'em out for a tour. Let's say 10.30, Friday 11th, eh?'

In essence the woods weren't quite as bad as they first appeared. They had suffered from years of poor management, or more precisely no management, but predominantly they were in good health. The major problem was the mess resulting from gale damage, the timber lying flat or at odd angles allowing the undergrowth to run riot. Fortunately only scattered areas had been affected but somehow it tinged the whole picture in Sir Charles' mind.

'Do these chaps ride?' asked Sir Charles. 'If so we can go round by horse.'

'I really haven't a clue, I'm afraid, Sir Charles. I never thought to ask.'

'Never mind. I don't suppose the one from London would anyway,' he mused.

The baronet held some odd views on any matter concerning London, mostly quite unfathomable although occasionally astute. No one who worked or lived there, he deemed, understood the countryside. It was no use pointing out that many country people might work in the city, may even live there for a while especially when younger. He was adamant. They knew nothing about it and as far as he was concerned the best conservation policy meant 'a bloody tall fence round the outskirts to keep 'em all in'.

To some extent he had a point. Politicians incurred his greatest wrath. Ridiculous laws, bureaucracy and meddling with countryside issues were cast-iron proof of their idiocy. Sir Charles would refuse point blank to attend any function if a member of parliament had also been invited. He blamed them for the downfall of the country.

'When my father was a young man in the 1920s,' he often reminded me, 'nearly a quarter – a quarter, d'you hear? – of the world's population lived under the British flag. Now we've got this idiot of a prime minister we've lost the Celts and he is trying to tie us up with the bloody Krauts. The Krauts of all people. They've tried to get us twice before you know, now they're getting in the back door and this bloody man's left it open for them. It's nothing less than treason.'

Unfortunately for Mr Sullivan's hopes of winning the contract, he worked for his firm's London office. Despite my revelations that he was a farmer's son and had inherited a useful 500 Hampshire acres it made no difference.

'He works in London so there's no hope he'll sit astride a horse,' Sir Charles stated forcefully.

It was a shame really as the ride through the Frampton woods was an unbelievable joy. When I had taken the job Sir Charles made it clear that he liked his agent to ride on the estate. My own horse, Grehan, was at Cordwainers but

Sir Charles owned a small stud of half a dozen mares, a stallion and a few hunters which were kept in the Victorian stable block on the east side of the Hall. He bred his horses for racing and the grooms were perfectly happy to saddle up a horse for me any time I wanted to take one out on the estate. Sometimes, Sir Charles and I would ride out together to inspect something or other in a remote area. By preference however, I would ride alone, savouring the solitude and closeness to nature. Each season had its charms and there was nowhere better to discover them than in the thousand acres of woodlands dotted around the estate.

I was to learn that no one season was more special than another but spring was inevitably the most uplifting. The warm air touched the earth, the life-giving soil upon which it all depended. Trees would blossom and break into leaf, clothing the dark brown skeletons of winter. The birds and animals appeared invigorated by the new growth of food and wild flowers burst into bloom, filling the air with their scent. Riding a horse through the bluebell woods in late April, the unbroken purple carpet was an aromatic delight greater than one could ever experience in a florist's or perfumery.

As spring grew into summer the delicate young leaves of the trees filled out providing a welcome cool canopy under which one could escape the heat of the day. My horse, tossing his head and flicking his tail to brush away the flies, would walk sedately along the grassy tracks through the woods. Out in the open country the fields were overflowing with beauty, the crops standing tall and plentiful across the rolling landscape as far as the eye could see. Cattle gathered in groups under the massive ancient oaks that stood in clumps in the park. Even the thundering of the horse's hooves cantering over the centuries-old turf would not rouse them from their midday siesta.

Like a pregnant young woman channelling the nourishment into her unborn child, the bellies of the fields filled as the summer wore on and in late July the harvesting would begin. The barley, having ripened to a light golden colour, was the first to be gathered, followed by the wheat. Late summer and early autumn gave the freedom to ride over the stubble, mile after mile of uncluttered countryside, broken only by hedges and woodland, was there for the taking. The colours would change again. The gold of the harvest echoed from the trees as their leaves turned an astonishing array of browns, reds, yellows and gold. Having given birth to a new generation in the spring, nurtured it through the heady days of summer, relinquishing it in the harvest of the autumn, the living countryside prepared for its winter rest.

There was a crispness about the morning air as autumn drew to a close. Fields now ploughed and drilled seemed dormant. The trees finally let go of their leaves and reappeared as skeletons against the sky. The smell of wood smoke drifted across from the village as fires were lit in the cottages and the rustle of leaves underfoot gave way to the crunch of the first frosts blanketing the countryside.

Even the harshness of winter held a beauty. The sharp air was invigorating, cock pheasants flew from the horse's path and often in the distance the thrilling sound of a hunting horn and braying hounds floated across the valleys.

I was always aware that my work on the estate gave me the great privilege of an insight into nature's mysteries and counted my blessings for that. Sometimes I would be outside, even under grey blankets of cloud that spread relentlessly across the horizon, with heavy rain pouring down. To feel the fresh water beating down on one's face was as important as the heat of the sun burning one's cheeks. The closeness to nature and feeling the most basic and essential elements of life was a joy. Yes, Sir Charles was right. City dwellers were at a disadvantage.

Yet there was no evidence of any sense of inferiority when Messrs Sullivan and East arrived at the Hall for their visit. They were both heartily full of enthusiasm, especially at Sir Charles' invitation to coffee in the house.

I was waiting for them with Sir Charles in the library when they arrived. A car had slowly crunched across the gravel in front of the house and about ten minutes later there was a knock on the door.

'Come in,' said Sir Charles.

'Mr Sullivan and Mr East for you, Sir Charles,' announced Hole.

'Ah, yes, good morning, good morning,' the baronet responded. 'Do come along in. How do you do. You know James Aden of course.'

Everyone shook hands rather formally and Sir Charles gestured for them to sit down. The library was an enormous room, lined with oak bookcases but also adorned with some seriously important works of art. Most prepossessing of all was a magnificent Rembrandt above the ornate marble mantelpiece, reputedly valued at more that the house itself.

'We'll take our coffee in the Grand Salon, Hole, at eleven o'clock, please,' declared Sir Charles. 'I want to show these gentlemen the estate maps beforehand.'

At one end of the room, Sir Charles had a detailed map of the estate permanently laid across a billiards table.

It seemed rather a waste of such a grand table but when I had suggested that I get the estate carpenter to make up a trestle table for the map, it had been declared an unnecessary expense. Besides, Sir Charles had said, there was another billiards table in the billiards room.

He had a bit of a thing about this map and I considered it

to be rather like a personalised Monopoly game. Sir Charles had made small wooden models that represented various things going on around the estate. A little red house for example, would be positioned where cottage renovations were being carried out. A green one meant work on a new farm building. Each farm had its symbols for stocking – a sheep, cow or pig as reality decreed. It seemed an archaic way of looking at the business but Sir Charles was passionate about keeping it up to date.

The guests seemed more interested in the Rembrandt than Sir Charles' map. However, they dutifully followed him over to the table so that he could show them the estate woodlands.

'All the woods are painted green,' he explained. 'See here, here, here and so on. Quite well scattered, aren't they?'

'Indeed,' replied Mr Sullivan, 'and varying greatly in size.'

'Yes, they do. This here,' Sir Charles said, pointing, 'is Brett Forest. It's the largest at about 300 acres. We'll go up there after coffee.'

I hovered in the background as they feigned fascination in his model and watched Monty, one of the poodles, wipe its bottom across a valuable Persian carpet.

There was a knock on the door and Hole announced that coffee was ready in the Salon.

'Jolly good, Hole. We're on our way now,' said Sir Charles, leading the way.

The Grand Salon was situated towards the far end of the house, quite a walk from the library. Every so often Sir Charles would stop at one of the many paintings that lined the walls and say something about it.

'Canaletto, Titian, Gainsborough, Van Dyck,' and so it went on.

The Salon itself had been built to impress. A large gracious room, albeit somewhat ostentatious, it overlooked the grand sweep at the front of the house. Huge floor to ceiling sash windows let in an abundance of light illuminating yet another collection of masterpieces. The furniture, mainly French from the Louis XV period, was as notable as the art. Although it was a beautiful room it was hardly relaxing, even though the baronet's poodles did their best to lend it an air of informality.

The two land agents asked about the arrangements for the house being open to the public.

'No, no. It's not open to the public, you know,' Sir Charles informed them.

They looked surprised, as well they might.

'Normally with a place this size and all the treasures in it, it would be open to visitors,' ventured Mr Sullivan rashly.

Sir Charles looked aghast. 'Good God,' he gasped, 'and have the great unwashed in here,' which effectively closed that avenue of conversation.

'I think we'd better get on and have a look at these woods, Sir Charles, we've got quite a lot of ground to cover,' I suggested.

'Absolutely, James. I'll get Hole to bring the car round.'

I looked at him in surprise as he tugged the bell cord by the fireplace.

'Your car, Sir Charles? I rather thought we'd be going in my Land Rover.'

'It's got no windows in the back,' he said, 'and no seats come to that. It will be much more comfortable in mine. Ah, Hole, there you are, could you bring the car round please.'

'Of course, Sir Charles,' he said. 'Will you be requiring the chains?'

'Oh, very much so,' Sir Charles replied. 'We'll wait for you here.'

Despite the eighth baronet's enormous wealth – just one painting would be worth more than the average man would earn in a lifetime – he was infamously reluctant to spend money on, as he put it, 'new-fangled technology'. The lack of telephones was one irritating example, his car was another.

The senior partner of Wright, Coke and Co. who had travelled down from London to be greeted by the baronet in his massive pile of a house, stuffed with priceless collections of paintings and furniture, might reasonably have expected Hole to draw up at the great south door in a Range Rover or some other upmarket four-wheel drive. What actually arrived was a green Morris Traveller clanking across the gravel with snow chains on its rear wheels.

The two men made no move towards it until Sir Charles exclaimed loudly, 'Well here we are then. Come on, dogs.' Turning towards me enquiringly, I just shrugged my shoulders. I was used to Sir Charles' eccentricities.

Sir Charles had bought the vehicle in 1972 and I suppose at the time it was a perfectly acceptable shooting brake quite adequate for estate use. Now, however, it had, to all extents and purposes, been superseded by more advanced technology. The exposed wooden frame and its cubed shape resembled a motorised chicken coop. Electric windows, central locking and reclining seats were not luxuries to impress Sir Charles. It didn't even have a radio. I remembered travelling with Sir Charles in someone's Range Rover on a hot afternoon when the driver had apologised about the lack of air conditioning.

'I'm afraid it's broken,' the man had said.

'Well, do what I do,' barked Sir Charles.

'What's that?'

'Open the bloody windows.'

I had been rather surprised when I had first arrived on the estate to find that it was the only vehicle up at the Hall. It would have been normal for there to have been at least a Land Rover to use on the muddy tracks but Sir Charles made do with a set of snow chains, saying him the expense of another car.

I sat in the front having volunteered to open the gates. The other two were wedged in the back with the poodles slobbering down their necks. After the grandeur of the big house events had taken a downward turn.

We made good headway on our tour despite the car getting stuck at regular intervals. The chains were only of limited use. Usually everyone would have to dismount and with Sir Charles' foot rammed down on the accelerator, we would push until the car was free again. By the end of the trip everyone bar the baronet was coated in mud. Our two visitors though had plenty of information with which to prepare a report on the woods.

I was rather relieved to get home and back to some normal behaviour. Perhaps I could spend an hour or two doing something useful on the farm.

'Sophie,' I shouted. 'Have you or anyone moved the ewes into Long Meadow today?'

I was standing in the kitchen at Cordwainers making a pot of tea and had noticed that the sheep were still in the front field by the drive. We followed a fairly strict routine of rotating the grazing around the farm which lessened the worm cycle to which overgrazed sheep are susceptible.

Sophie came through from the hall carrying an old leather suitcase. By the way she was struggling I guessed that it was heavy.

'No, I haven't got round to it yet and I forgot to ask Bert when I saw him. Sorry. Can you do it? Jess needs a run anyway.'

'No problem. What on earth is in that case?'

'It's full of papers but I don't know what about. I found it in the attic.'

'Oh, no,' I said, 'you haven't started sorting out the stuff up there have you? I thought we were going to wait until the rest of the house was organised before we did that.'

There was enough clutter around the place without bringing more down from the attic.

'I know, I know. I just wanted to have a look at the odd thing here and there. It is absolutely crammed with interesting bits and pieces. I found some gorgeous chairs which could be re-covered,' she enthused.

'What do we need more chairs for?' I asked. 'We've already got more than we need.'

'Well we don't need them as such,' she explained, 'but as they're there we might as well look at them.'

I shrugged my shoulders. Sophie was obsessed with trying to sort out all the things that we had inherited from Uncle William with the house. I reckoned that we had years to do it and as long as the main parts of the house were in good shape the rest could wait.

I swigged back my tea and grabbed a shepherd's crook from the collection of sticks beside the door.

'I'm going to go and move these ewes,' I informed her. 'Do you want to come with me?'

'No, I'm going to look through this and then start cooking some supper. Can you check the lambs in Dip Field while you're over that way. Thanks.'

I was just about to leave when the telephone rang. Sophie

answered it. I could hear who it was from across the room. George Pratt from Rumshott.

After the introductory pleasantries, Sophie said, 'Well, he's here, if you want a word, but it would be lovely to see you.'

She handed the receiver to me, which I held at arm's length.

'Hallo, George,' I said, 'how nice to hear from you. Haven't seen you for ages.'

'Well you're just about to,' he shouted. 'Got a meeting in your part of the woods soon and thought I'd drop in.'

'Excellent. Come for lunch.' We checked dates and happily there didn't seem to be a problem.

'Damn meeting with some conservation group that Lord Rumshott has got involved with. Some ridiculous scheme to do with breeding bats.'

'Oh,' I replied. 'His lordship's still finding little projects then?'

'Incessantly,' George shouted. 'And they get more bizarre by the week. I'll tell you about it when I see you. Looking forward to it,' and the line went dead.

'Nothing's changed there then.' Sophie laughed. 'Actually, it'll be fun to see him won't it?'

'Yes, it will,' I agreed. 'But now I'd better deal with these sheep.'

I collected Jess from her kennel who went mad with excitement. If I was carrying a crook she knew that meant working the sheep and that was her sole joy in life. She was a good working dog and I had often thanked the day that William had offered to take her when we left Harbottle.

Bramble had followed me out and she came with us down to the field. However, as always she behaved rather pathetically as we neared the sheep and wouldn't come in.

When she had been a puppy one of the rams had taken a dislike to her and beaten her up, repeatedly butting her while she had tried to run away. There had been a lot of yelping. She would never be caught worrying sheep, that was for sure.

Jess meanwhile had cast far out along the hedge line scooping up the sheep as they dashed away from her. With half an eye on me and half on the ewes, she brought them towards me as I opened the gate to the adjoining field.

'Steady, Jess,' I shouted as they approached rather quickly. Too fast and some would miss the opening, scatty as they were. Inevitably one silly old bugger tried to get through the wrong side of the gatepost and hit the fence with a twang of stretching wire. There was a brief struggle as Jess took the opportunity to nip its hind legs before it shot off like a stone from a catapult. Funny animals, sheep, I always thought, incredibly stupid and stubborn, and either happily grazing or dead. There didn't seem to be much in between.

Once the sheep had disappeared, Bramble rejoined us and we walked off towards the far side of the farm. The lambs, recently weaned, were in a field behind Hall Wood, a beautiful ancient woodland at the top of the hill. It was a lovely walk along wide grass rides through oak and ash trees with hazel coppice growing underneath. Sophie had arranged for some forestry contractors to cut an area of the coppice which was normal forestry practice and I wanted to see how they were progressing. It wasn't the ideal time of year to be doing it but they had offered us a good enough price to persuade us to let them start. With the constant pressure on farm incomes it was useful to have the money. I was happily minding my own business, letting the dogs run on ahead, when I looked up to see a couple of people poking about in the area we had just felled. Although there was a footpath that ran alongside the wood, there were no rights of way through it. The dogs saw them too and ran over barking inquisitively.

'These dogs should be on leads,' the man shouted at me, the woman with him trying to use him as a shield.

Bloody cheek, I thought and continued walking towards them, not replying. When I was near enough not to need to shout I asked them what they were doing.

'We've come to look at this destruction here,' the man said, the woman nodding furiously. 'This lovely wood being cut down.'

'Well, you've no right to be in here,' I said, 'and it's no concern of yours anyway.'

'Who are you?' he asked.

'I own the woods,' I explained. 'They're private. Where are you from? I don't recognise you?'

They weren't locals, I could tell that by the presence of some maps, compasses and unidentifiable items festooned about their persons.

'We're ramblers from Norwich,' the woman told me in a similar manner to which she might have said her husband had been awarded the OBE. 'We were on our way back to our car and saw this. We thought we should report it.'

'To who?'

There was a silence. 'Well, to whoever should know, I suppose. Perhaps the council.'

Interfering busybodies. The world was swamped with them now. I considered myself a reasonable person, left others to get on with their own lives and didn't take kindly to those that meddled in mine.

'You know absolutely nothing about woodlands. Well, despite my inclination to tell you to clear off, I'll explain what's going on here provided that next time you wander about the countryside poking your noses into things, you listen to the reasoning behind it.'

The woman gasped and I suspected I had rather overdone it but as they didn't immediately stalk off I told them how coppiced woodlands were cut down on a rotation of between fifteen and twenty-five years. Not only was that good for timber production but also, I went on, it was vital to maintain a healthy balance of plant and bird life.

Much to my surprise they appeared quite grateful for the information and we parted on very friendly terms. It was, I reflected, symptomatic of the increasing conflict between those of us who lived and worked in the country and those who used it as their playground. And it was likely to get worse. It seemed as though if the government had its way the whole place would be turned into a giant theme park with a few animals to stroke, cared for by the last remaining peasants, dressed in regulation Eurosmocks, sucking chemically cleansed pieces of straw.

Eventually I reached the lambs and had a good look through them. My main concern was checking for fly – when the eggs laid around the tails hatched into maggots and fed on the flesh of the animals. It was the most unpleasant of all a shepherd's tasks, dealing with a fly-blown lamb. All seemed well and the dogs and I made our way back to the house having enjoyed a slightly unusual outing.

Sophie and I were eating supper in the kitchen when the phone rang. The damned thing never seemed to stop.

'I'll get it, you finish yours,' Sophie offered. 'Are you in?'

'Oh, it depends, um, say I'll ring back.'

She picked it up and answered. There was some squawking at the other end.

'Hallo, Brigadier Hand,' she said. I was shaking my head violently. 'James is out, I'm afraid.'

More squawking.

'I don't know where, on the farm somewhere . . .'

'What barn?'

'. . . No, I never said barn. I'm not following you, Brigadier.'

'A fence judge at the hunter trials.'

'Yes, I'll pass the message on.'

She replaced the receiver. 'Did you get that? He's so difficult to understand. He wants you to fence judge at the Pony Club hunter trials in September. You'd better ring him back later.'

'We can both offer, can't we? It'll be quite a fun day actually.'

'Yeah, I'm happy to help. Besides, if I don't, Mrs Hand will be asking me to make a cake or something for the fundraising stall.'

I laughed. 'Yes, do you remember the fudge you made for the stall at that do they had in the square? It was like trying to eat little slabs of concrete.'

'Hey, you, it wasn't that bad.' Sophie put her arms around my neck and kissed me. 'Was it?'

'Mrs Hand cracked a tooth on it. You must remember!'

'Shut up. She's just got weak teeth. I'm going to make some coffee,' she said, letting go.'Want some?'

'Thanks. I'll ring the old boy back while you're doing that, then we can go and watch some television. I could do with an evening dossing about.'

I went into the study to ring the Brigadier.

'James Aden here,' I said, exaggerating each syllable for his benefit.

'Ah, Aden, good of you to ring back so promptly, old chap. Did Susie pass the message on?'

'Sophie, you mean.'

'What?'

'My wife's name is Sophie, Brigadier.'

'Is it? Well I suppose you'd know. Anyway, did you get the message about the hunter trials?'

'Yes, I did. I'm very happy to help and so is Sophie. She said she'd rather that than make fudge again!' I joked.

'No, no,' the Brigadier barked. 'The girl's got it wrong. I asked if you'd judge, not make fudge. That's a woman's job.'

'No, I know. Yes, I'll help,' I repeated.

There was a silence from the Brigadier's end. Then he continued, 'I don't know what you're talking about. What's yes and no. Yes and no what?'

I sometimes wondered whether the man took delight in being obtuse, he was extraordinarily difficult to talk to on the telephone.

'Yes, I will fence judge at the hunter trials, Brigadier,' I bellowed clearly.

'Oh, good fellow,' he bellowed back. 'Knew I could count on you. While you're on, can I ask you to let Sir Charles know the date. He's letting us use the park as normal providing that we don't make too much of a mess at the gymkhana. That's coming up soon you know.'

'Yes, I'll let him know. And as I was trying to say earlier, Sophie would be willing to judge as well.'

'Marvellous. I'll tell the wife to expect some of Susie's fudge. Jolly decent of her to go to the trouble.'

It wasn't worth the effort going through the rigmarole again. I'd leave it until I saw him in person.

Chapter 10

I spent most of the following morning sitting at my desk in the estate office contemplating what Wright, Coke and Co. might suggest. As we were not all that busy and I had a slight headache I decided to get some fresh air and stretch my legs.

'Is there anything I can get you?' I called to Anne as she busily typed some letters. 'I shan't be long. No more than half an hour, anyway.'

'Would you mind getting some cheese sandwiches, the ones with low fat spread, from the bakers?' she asked.

After walking briskly for twenty minutes my head was now clear and I was beginning to feel confident that dealing with Wright, Coke and Co. would not be a problem. As I turned back into the square I remembered that I had promised Anne her sandwiches so headed towards the bakers, thinking that I may as well get some bread for Sophie and myself as well. There were a few customers in the shop so I took my place at the counter and awaited my turn. I was just pondering the relative merits of a white tin compared to a Danish bloomer when I noticed that the girl from Le Champignon was on my left. Dressed casually out of her waitress' uniform, she appeared even more attractive. Her long fair hair flowed freely down her back, tucked carelessly behind her ears and a few tendrils of golden plaits brushed her flawless face.

I waited what seemed like an age while the customers ahead of me were served their bread and as much local gossip as they could swallow until finally I was at the head of the queue.

'Good morning, Hilda,' I greeted the baker's wife.

'Morning, Mr Aden,' she replied, and the old ladies in the queue chirped in with her like a chorus of finches.

'One low-fat spread cheese sandwich and a small white tin, please, Hilda.'

'Certainly, Mr Aden. 'As she prepared the sandwich in front of me she spoke again. 'Have you heard the latest about James Owen, Mr Aden?'

'Well, no I haven't, Hilda. But I'm afraid I haven't got time to gossip.'

Hilda looked up sharply. 'That'll be £1.70 then, Mr Aden,' she said frostily.

It was an irony of Frampton that not wanting to gossip was considered the height of bad manners.

As I turned to leave the baker's I heard a vaguely familiar voice call out.

''Allo, sir. I 'opes you enjoyed your meal the other night.' The girl smiled at me, searching for recognition in my face.

'Oh, fine, thank you, yes,' I mumbled.

'Have you . . .?' we both started together.

'Sorry, after you,' I said.

'No, no, es all right. Es not important. You want to say something?'

'No, I was just passing the time of day really. What were you going to say?' I asked.

She shrugged and laughed.

'I forget now. Es not, no, it es no matter.'

'Oh.' There was another slightly awkward little pause.

'I haven't seen you around the village,' I tried again. 'Have you been here long?'

'No. This es true. I have been living here for a few weeks only. Mine Dupont is my aunt. My mother has arranged for me to work 'ere,' she explained in her broken English.

'Oh, I see. You still live with your parents?' I asked, half expecting her to say that she lived with her racing driver boyfriend on the Côte D'Azur.

'Yes, and my two sisters,' she replied.

'Where do they live?' I asked.

'They live in France.'

'Yes, I sort of assumed that,' I said. 'Whereabouts? What part?'

'Er, part? I not understand what you mean.'

'Um, area, region. What region do they come from?'

'Ah, pardon. My English es not too good yet. I must practice but I live here only a short time so I 'ave many words to learn.'

'Well I think you speak it very well already,' I enthused.

'Oh, thank you,' she said, blushing slightly, fluttering her eyelids almost imperceptibly. 'But to answer you, my family lives in a region called Le Haute Savoie. Es in the montagnes.'

'Oh, I know that area,' I said. 'I go skiing in Val D'Isere.'

'Val D'Isere. Ah, se best ski station in se world! I love Val D'Isere.' She paused. 'And you, where you live? In se village?'

'No, I live on a farm outside the village,' I answered.

'I see. And your work for that what es it?' she asked.

'I'm Sir Charltes Buckley's agent,' I replied.

'Sir Charles' . . . agent? I do not understand agent.'

'He's Sir Charles' manservant, dear,' interjected Hilda, who had apparently been listening to our entire conversation.

'Oh,' the girl looked at me doubtfully. 'You are a man friend?'

'No, it's not what you think,' I hastened to assure her. 'My relationship with Sir Charles is professional.'

'He pays you?' she asked, surprise etched into her voice.

'Oh, dear, we've got this conversation in a bit of a muddle.' I tried to explain once more when the shop door flew open, crashing back against the wall.

'Mr Aden, come quickly,' gasped Mrs Birch from the Anne of Cleves. 'Fred Turner's just fallen off his bike. He's lying in the road with blood pouring from his head.'

I hovered uncertainly, not wanting to leave the conversation in its present condition. Much as I did not want Fred Turner's injuries to worsen because I had not helped, nor did I want this charming French girl to think that I was anything other than a red-blooded Englishman.

Mrs Birch grabbed my arm. 'Come on, he's dying, quick.'

There was nothing for it but to be dragged across the square to where old Fred was lying on the cobbles. A small crowd had gathered and it was difficult at first to see what had happened.

'Has someone called an ambulance?' I shouted.

'Yes, I've done that,' said Mrs Birch. 'Ten minutes, they said.'

'Someone get a blanket will they, but don't move him. Just cover him up till it gets here.'

Poor old Fred. It was distressing seeing him lying there unconscious. It looked as though he'd ridden straight into the memorial cross. The front wheel of his bicycle was bent. Goodness knows why. The cross had been there for 500 years and he'd never hit it before.

Fred Turner was an estate pensioner. He had spent five decades as a gardener at the Hall and now lived in a cottage at the bottom of Hill Street. It had been an unusual choice of retirement home for him to take as all the village shops were at the top of a steep hill. He did however get a large garden and that was what mattered to him. Not only did he want to continue gardening, but he also wanted the space to keep his bantams.

While the blanket was being fetched, he started to come round. His old wizened face twitched as he tried to recollect his surroundings. I knelt down beside him.

'It's all right, Fred, take it easy. You've fallen off your bike,' I explained.

He struggled to sit up and some eager hands lent support, wedging him against the old stone cross.

'Cor blimey,' he muttered, 'that was a bad do.'

'Yes, you've cut the side of your head and got concussion but otherwise seem okay. Just stay still – we've called an ambulance.'

He started to try to stand up. 'I don't need no bloody ambulance,' he retorted. 'I ain't a basket case yet.'

'I know,' I said, 'but it's best if you go and have a check-up. It'll be fine, I'm sure. You'll be back in a couple of hours.'

As it turned out he was detained in the local hospital over night but seemed quite cheerful about it when he rang the estate office late that afternoon.

'I'm fine 'ere for t'night, thank you, Mr Aden. But I 'ave a worry needs attending to if you'd be so kind.'

'Of course, Fred. What is it?' I asked.

'It's me bantams. They'll need shutting in t'coop before dark and feedin' in t'morning. Hoary next door'll do it but he's not on t'phone.'

'I'll go down and see him,' I assured him, 'and we'll see you back here tomorrow.'

I was about to leave when the telephone rang again.

'Turner 'ere again, Mr Aden. Sorry to bother you. Tell Hoary 'e can 'ave t'eggs but not the speckled ones. They're to put under a broody.'

'Right, I'll tell him. I'm going down now.'

I was walking down Hill Street to see old Hoary when a car drew up alongside me. It was Monsieur Dupont.

'Excuse me, Mr Aden,' he said. 'I wonder if you could call in at number ten. My staff there tell me there is a problem with the hot water. It is quite urgent as you can imagine.'

'Okay, I'll pop over in about twenty minutes. Will someone be there?'

'Yes, for about another half an hour, after that they'll be at work. Thank you.'

I knocked on Hoary's door and told him about Fred and the bantams.

'You'll 'ave a cup o' tea with me, Misser Aden,' he shouted, deaf from years of shooting rabbits.

'That's kind, Hoary, but I've got to be in the High Street in ten minutes. Another time maybe.'

'Suit yourself then,' he bellowed and slammed the door. He wasn't being rude, it was just his manner.

Normally I wouldn't go and look at this sort of problem but would send for the estate plumber instead. But as the matter was urgent and it was unlikely that the plumber would be able to come for several hours it made more sense to go and see for myself.

Number ten was an old Tudor cottage crammed between an antiques shop and the newsagent. Although the frontage to the street was narrow the cottage was deceptively large as it included the rooms above the adjoining shops. It was ideal for Monsieur Dupont's staff.

I rang the bell and waited. No one came so I rang again.

This time I heard a babble of agitated French voices and a young man of about my own age opened the door.

'Oui?'

'Bonjour – hallo. My name's James Aden. I'm from the estate office. Monsieur Dupont has asked me to look at your hot-water problem,' I explained.

The man looked uncomprehendingly at me.

'You have no hot water,' I tried again. 'Pas de l'eau chaud.'

He rattled off a load of French and looked expectantly at me but I hadn't a clue what he was on about.

'Do you speak English?' I asked.

'Wait, please,' he said and disappeared. A few moments later he reappeared. 'You are Sir Charles' man, yes?' he asked, a faint smile creasing his lips.

'Yes,' I barked, now fed up with the unnecessary delay.

He shouted into the depths of the house and a moment later the girl whose acquaintance I had made earlier appeared. She was clad solely in a large bath towel, her wet hair falling in ringlets over her shoulders.

I gulped. 'Oh, hallo again. Sorry I've disturbed you but Monsieur Dupont tells me you have no hot water.'

She smiled, oblivious to the embarrassment her near nakedness was having on me.

'Es you again. Es right. We 'ave no hot water. Just now I 'ave cold shower.' She laughed. 'Es very cold, I know!'

'Can I come in and have a look, do you think?' I asked.

'You?'

'Yes, if that's okay.'

'Ah, I see. You es the, what you say, the man for the waterworks.'

'You mean plumber.' I smiled.

By this point I was just about ready to give up any hope of untangling the wires of our communication. If she wanted to think of me as a gay plumber then so be it. I just prayed that her misguided thoughts would not turn into local gossip. Over time even inaccurate gossip came to be regarded as the gospel in Frampton.

It occurred to me that Sophie would not appreciate late night calls from people wanting their pipes looked at so I doubled my resolve to clear up the misunderstanding. I followed her into the kitchen where she pointed out the boiler. The kitchen was a complete mess with stacks of dirty plates in the sink, pans all over the work tops and a pile of unwashed clothes on the floor.

I looked at it all. 'It's a bit of a mess in here, isn't it?' I said. 'Doesn't anyone bother washing up?'

'Normally es okay, but with no 'ot water es difficult.'

'Yes, sorry, stupid of me,' I muttered.

I turned the hot-water tap on at the sink but the boiler failed to fire up. Checking the boiler controls I saw that both the settings for hot water and the central heating were in the off position. I switched the water one on and tried the tap again. This time the boiler roared into life.

The girl clapped her hands together and smiled.

'Ah, you es clever,' she shrieked happily.

'No, not really.' I laughed. 'Look, this switch needs to be kept here all the time. Then you'll always have hot water.'

She perched on a stool, her towel clutched tightly around her chest but with plenty of shapely bare leg on view.

'You es good with the plumbing,' she continued ecstatically.

'What is your name?' I asked her.

'Isobel,' she said, smiling.

'Well, it's nice to meet you, Isobel,' I replied, my voice rising as I spoke. 'I'm glad I could fix this for you but I have to admit it was luck. I'm not a plumber, you see, just come to find out what was wrong and try to help.'

'I try to 'elp you too,' she said, 'in Le Champignon. You had ze sauce in your hair and so I keep doing thees.' She ran her hands through her hair. 'I try to show you but you just keeps looking at me.'

Chapter 11

The next morning, Gail came panting into my office. Despite her penchant for chasing after men, usually younger than her thirty-five years, she was a rather large lady. She went to the trouble of dyeing her hair peroxide blonde and wearing bras that exhibited the relevant assets to their best advantage, but a slim figure was beyond her reach.

'Have you met the man that's moved into the Old Rectory?' she gasped. 'He moved in yesterday.'

'No,' I replied. 'He's moved in at last has he?'

The Old Rectory now belonged to the estate and was one of the most expensive lettable houses in the village. The long-term lease, which I wasn't entirely happy with, had been arranged by the previous land agent, but for some unknown reason it had taken the new tenant months to move in.

'He's a young bloke with loads of money,' she continued with excitement. 'Made a fortune out of the Internet. Got his own company, I'm told.'

'Oh, right,' I muttered. 'I guessed whoever was moving in must have some cash. He's paying way over the odds.'

'Yes, he's got all sorts of plans to do it up. He wants to convert some of the stables into offices, take a wall out here, extend the garden, loads of things.'

'Well, it's not up to him. He can come and ask if he likes but I doubt Sir Charles will agree to it.'

I expect he's also a target for your sexual frustration, I thought to myself. Gail's relationship with the groom had proved short-lived, so it seemed that she was once again on the man trail.

'Is he single or married?' I asked.

'Oh, very much single, I'm told. Bit of a fast one, likes his women, sports cars, designer clothes, all that sort of thing.'

'Well, he'll certainly stick out like a sore thumb around here, won't he?'

'Oh, I think it's all rather exciting. Bit of new life. Spice things up a bit. I hope he comes down to the Anne of Cleves.'

The Anne of Cleves was the focal point for most of the village social life. Much of Gail's information came via the pub and I suspected that if one watched the doors studiously over an evening a lot of clandestine village goings-on would be observed.

'I expect he'll soon be in there trying out the local,' I said, hoping that Gail wasn't about to embark upon another mission. We hadn't heard much about the groom which was unusual as she liked to keep Anne up to date on all the details of her love life. They tended to be stormy relationships and the office reverberated between bursts of euphoria and bouts of sobbing.

The thoughts of Gail's romances made me reflect on a conversation I'd had with Sir Charles a month or so earlier concerning his heir and only child Sebastian. Despite Sir Charles' great wealth and position in society he had suffered a tragic personal life. He had married some fifty years ago an allegedly beautiful and charming young woman, Lady Catherine Edgeworth, the eldest daughter of the fifth duke of Sapperton. A debutante, an heiress in her own right and immensely admired for her quick wit and intelligence, she had produced Sebastian in their second year of marriage. Two years later, pregnant again, she had fallen from a horse whilst out hunting and broken her neck. Neither she, nor the unborn child, had survived.

Sir Charles, an emotionally private man, had never remarried even though he was one of the most eligible men in the country and had been pursued by plenty of bounty hunters. He had once said that Lady Catherine had been so perfect for him that he had accepted that he would never find anyone to equal her. He remained a widower and Sebastian was brought up an only child in a one-parent family. Inevitably in a formal household there were nannies but father and son were close. The unusual situation had undoubtedly had some effect on Sebastian. He was a bit strange. I don't think Sir Charles noticed because in some ways their oddities were similar but he did notice that Sebastian wasn't married. He had never even had a girl-friend. Sir Charles worried greatly about this because there was no eventual heir to the baronetcy, or indeed his fortune.

Having had a solitary childhood Sebastian was painfully shy. His chosen career had done little to take him into the big wide world as he had become a professor of anthropology at Cambridge University. I had discovered that the stuffed monkey in my office was something to do with a presentation he was due to give at his college.

Sir Charles worried greatly about the future and like most people in his position, the continuation of the family line was paramount. After Sir Charles' death everything would pass to Sebastian, and then what?

The discussion concerning Sebastian's lack of action in the reproduction area had been sparked off by a necessary revaluation of Sir Charles' assets. Apart from the 10,000 acres in Suffolk and the contents of the Hall, there was a sizeable share portfolio, 40,000 acres in Sutherland, a cattle ranch in Alberta and a block of property in Chelsea.

It was not surprising that his father worried. However, it was surprising, at least to me, that Sebastian drove around in a Reliant Robin. Even more bizarrely he'd converted it to accommodate his companion, Argonaut, an Irish wolfhound the size of a donkey. The unusual conversion had left the driver's seat intact but the rest of the interior was boarded over with timber and covered in dog blankets. I always thought it was a bit strange for a man worth about £250 million to drive around in what amounted to a large plastic dog bed. The explanation, apparently, was that he paid a reduced road tax.

He lived in a small house in Cambridge but returned to Frampton intermittently. I saw him occasionally but his reclusiveness prevented him taking much part in estate life. It was a tragic situation. Sir Charles wanted the three of us to meet and discuss what plans could be made for the future of the estate and I had duly arranged for us to spend a whole day together looking at the options during Sebastian's summer break.

Apart from that I had plenty of other work to do, most pressing was a rent review on Bush Farm, a large arable holding on the western edge of the estate. It was tenanted by a very successful, though aggressive, farmer called John Hopkins who firmly believed the rent should be reduced. I did not agree with him and our last meeting had not been productive. I had visited the farm in the spring when admittedly the place was looking its best. The crops and trees were filling out, the hedges were alive with bird life, indeed all 800 acres were bursting with the optimism of that time of year.

Bush Farm was an impressive place irrespective of the

quality of the farmer. A lime tree avenue led up to the symmetrical Georgian front of the house and a wide gravel sweep gave it a much grander air than that of a working farmhouse. A gleaming black Range Rover was parked by the porticoed entrance and as I had driven up a couple of Labradors had rushed out, barking furiously.

John Hopkins had come out to greet me. A man in his fifties, well built and fit, he took as much pride in his own appearance as he did in that of his farm. He had prospered and skilfully managed his resources in the good times to ensure that as farming incomes declined his lifestyle was not threatened. With two children at public school, a glamorous high-maintenance wife and his own interest in shooting he had a lot to support.

Farm rents are fixed on the basis of what the farm is worth, not what the farmer can afford. I knew this but Mr Hopkins seemed to think differently. He incessantly pleaded poverty and Suffolk farmers are very good at doing so even when surrounded by somewhat obvious trappings of wealth.

He showed me through into a new conservatory he'd had built the previous winter. It was an enormous great thing with a marble floor and opened out on to a swimming pool.

'Well, it's been a difficult year again for farming,' he began. 'Sometimes I wonder whether it's worth going on with the job at all, you know, James.'

'Oh, surely it's not that bad, John,' I said looking around me. 'I know it's getting harder but there's still a profit in it for efficient chaps like you.'

'It's a lot of hard graft for little reward nowadays,' he went on. 'Goodness only knows where it'll take us.'

'Well, I think provided one is realistic about costs and

future income, most people will survive. Especially if they've got a reasonable acreage like you have here.'

'You've hit the nail on the head there young man,' he remarked, pointing a finger at me. 'Realistic about costs, you say, and yet you're asking me to pay the same rent as for the past three years. It's got to come down if I'm to survive.'

'I knew you'd disagree,' I said, 'but this farm is still capable of sustaining the present rent, John. It's a good farm, productive clay soils excellent for wheat. You've got sugar beet quota, modern buildings put up by the landlord, an attractive house. There's even income from those old poultry sheds now that they're converted to light industrial units. There's a lot going for it.'

'You say all that, James, and I don't disagree that this is a handy sort of farm. But the point is, no matter how good it is or how efficient we are at farming it, I'm struggling to make ends meet.'

At that point a white Mercedes convertible swept past the side of the house towards the garages.

'Ah, that'll be the missus,' he declared. 'She'll make us a pot of coffee when she comes in.'

'That would be nice,' I said. 'Getting back to the point though, we have got a bit of a problem. I just can't recommend to Sir Charles that we accept a rent reduction.'

'Hallo!' shouted his wife as she approached us across the lawn. 'Lovely to see you. Gorgeous day, isn't it?'

I stood up. 'Hallo, yes, it's lovely. You've been playing tennis by the look of it,' I remarked.

'Yes, always have a ladies' four on Thursdays. Anyway, I expect you two would like some coffee.'

'That'd be nice love,' said her husband. 'You had a good game by the sound of it.'

'Yes, thanks, darling. Marjorie was there. She seems much happier since Giles has come home.'

She turned to me.

'You know Adam and Marjorie Appleyard, don't you? He's one of the partners in the vets at Flixton. They've had such an ordeal with their youngest son Giles. He took up with a girl from London that they never really liked, then moved in with her much against their wishes, only for him to find out she was a prostitute.'

'Oh dear,' I commented. 'How . . . er, awkward.'

'More than bloody awkward,' butted in John, 'the scandal of it all nearly killed poor old Marjorie. Stopped going out, gave up tennis, didn't play the organ on Sunday anymore. Was a right bad do.'

'Thank goodness Giles saw sense,' continued Mrs Hopkins. 'He's back now and the latest is that he's going to take up his place at university in the autumn. Anyway, let me get the coffee.'

She disappeared into the kitchen and our discussion returned to the gloom and doom of farming. By the time we'd finished coffee we were no further forward and John had suggested that I talk to his agent. His land agent happened to be Tony East who was a reasonable enough man so I readily agreed. I pointed out that he was about to become involved in some work for the estate but John Hopkins had no qualms about any conflict of interest.

'The man's as straight as a die,' he assured me. 'Talk to him about it.'

My visit had been about two months previously and nothing more had happened. I felt I would have to press Tony East into a meeting and dictated a letter suggesting some dates.

'Anne, would you type this for me?' I asked, giving her the tape.

'Of course,' she said. 'And have you got a moment to ring Mrs Ellis? She called again about her leaking roof, and also the new man at the Old Rectory rang. He wants to know if he can lease the field next door. He wants to extend his garden apparently.'

'Yes, I'll ring Mrs Ellis and, no, he can't have the field. Bit bloody impertinent. Gail said he only moved in yesterday.'

'She's rather excited about him,' Anne whispered. 'Between you and me I think she rather fancies him!'

'Oh, here we go again. I thought as much. I think we've got another drama about to unfold.'

'Well, you know what she's like once she gets her mind set on a bloke. And Trevor Castle's made millions out of the web world, no that's not it, world wide web, so he's quite a catch.'

'I know, I know,' I butted in, 'she's already told me all this. I'm going to ring Mrs Ellis.'

I strode back into my office. I hoped that this Trevor Castle wasn't going to stir the relatively calm waters. If he did it would inevitably end up as my lot to sort it out. It didn't help my frame of mind dealing with Mrs Ellis either. She was a moaner. She whinged and screeched with a pitch of voice that drilled straight into one's brain.

'Hallo, Mrs Ellis,' I said into the telephone. 'James Aden here at the estate office.'

'Who's that?' she replied, deaf as a post.

'James Aden at the estate office,' I shouted.

'The estate office,' she screeched. 'I want something done about me roof.'

'Why don't I come . . .'

'Let me finish,' she commanded. 'I've been asking for the

roof to be fixed for a year. I have been advised that unless it is fixed soon I must write to my solicitor.'

I kept hearing this nonsense about being 'advised', a recurring phrase that prefaced anything she ever said to us.

'I'll come and see you this afternoon,' I bellowed down the phone.

'You'll come this afternoon?' she cried.

'Yes.'

'Well that might not be convenient for me. You can't just come when you like.'

'Well, when would suit you?'

'I don't really know,' she said. 'What time would you come this afternoon?'

'Whenever you like.'

'What time did you say?'

'Any time you want. How about now?' I might as well get it over and done with before she drove me mad.

'You'll come now, will you?'

'Yes.'

'Is Mr Aden coming with you?'

'This is Mr Aden speaking.'

'Well, never mind, you come instead. What's your name?'

I gave up and put the phone down. It would be quicker to run over to her cottage where she might hear what I was saying.

She opened the door as far as the security chain would allow.

'Hallo, Mrs Ellis. James Aden here to look at your roof,' I said loudly.

'Oh, yes, wait a bit while I undo this door,' she replied. I waited for an age while she fiddled around with the thing.

When she eventually let me in, she explained, 'I'm very conscious about security,' she said. 'I'm a member of the

Neighbourhood Watch scheme.' She pointed at a little yellow sticker in the front window.

I knew she was involved in what I called the Nosy Neighbour scheme, one of the increasingly common and annoying interferences that the local council or someone had hit upon. To my mind any decent neighbour would automatically keep an eye out for any misdemeanours, it didn't need the bureaucracy of yet another army of do-gooders. It had amused me when there had been a change of tenants in the cottage next door to Mrs Ellis and she hadn't noticed for a month. It rather threw the value of the scheme into question.

'Tell me about the latest problem with your roof, Mrs Ellis. Where is it leaking now?'

'I'll show you,' she said and beckoned me to follow her out into the kitchen.

The back of the cottage was a single-storey Victorian extension and to be fair it had been leaking on and off for years. It was time the whole thing was re-roofed so I explained this to her.

'Well, I hope it won't cause a lot of mess,' she started. 'Only I can't cope with a lot of mess at my age.'

This was the dilemma I always had with her. Whichever way we went there was something wrong. If we didn't fix it, she complained. If we did then the disruption caused upset.

'Well, this time we must do the job properly once and for all. The builders will try not to disturb you too much but I'd like to get this done before the coming winter.'

'When you're my age you just can't cope,' she said again. 'I'm nearly ninety, you know. And I'm not very well, though I suppose I shouldn't complain. There's others worse off than me. Take my friend Mrs Jackson, can hardly walk now without a stick and she's not eighty-two. And then there's poor old George Prentice, got something wrong with his, you know, down below.'

I knew from past conversations that this dialogue could go on all afternoon so with a firm commitment to get on with the job I departed. Inevitably, with a policy of providing homes for life for estate workers there was a fair proportion of elderly tenants. Most of them were fascinating characters who livened up the life of the village. Somehow though, Mrs Ellis never did it for me.

Chapter 12

Soon after Sophie and I had moved to Cordwainers we had decided to join the local tennis club. The club was one of the few amenities in the village which meant it would be a good place to make new friends and get involved with the social side of the community. We played on Tuesday evenings when anybody who fancied a game could turn up and be guaranteed at least one set. Sophie and I were keen players and usually played through until dusk. While the club's membership spanked all age groups there was a decent number of players in their twenties and thirties and we had made some good friends. We would regularly go to the pub afterwards and make an evening of it.

On the Tuesday after I'd seen Mrs Ellis and dealt with a few other irritating minor problems, I had felt the need to release some frustration and played with more energy and style than usual, lunging deftly around the court much to the astonishment of the others. A little later as the light faded, we all wandered off to the Anne of Cleves. There was still enough warmth in the air to sit outside so we took our seats at a large round table. It was a good place to watch the world go by, in as much as it did in Frampton. Sophie particularly enjoyed socialising with our new friends and getting away from the farm for an evening. It was normally late by the time we got home to Cordwainers.

The following morning, for the second time in as many

days, I had to put up with Gail's excited chatter about the Old Rectory.

'I met Trevor Castle yesterday,' she babbled, 'he's really charming. Not at all what I expected.'

'What were you expecting?' I asked.

'Well, I thought he'd be flashy, you know sort of Essex boy made good.'

'Gold medallions on a hairy chest you mean?'

'Sort of – no a bit more classy than that but a bit rough around the edges if you know what I mean,' she faltered.

'I don't really, to be honest. Anyway I've got to get on. I'm sure I'll bump into him somewhere. Where did you meet him by the way?' Knowing Gail, I guessed she had engineered it.

'I was walking Charlie through the churchyard and Trevor was pottering about.' Charlie was her fat, aggressive little terrier, which always reminded me of a cocktail sausage on legs.

'Trevor, eh!' I probed.

'He's only, I don't know, mid- to late twenties, I can't call him Mr Castle, can I?' she justified.

'No, I suppose not,' I agreed, opening my office door. There was a mountain of paper on my desk. I paused.

'Did you get chatting to him then?'

'Briefly. I told him I worked in the estate office and he seemed quite interested in that.'

'I'll bet,' I remarked thoughtfully.

'Why do you say that?'

'I expect he might find it useful to have a contact within the estate, don't you?'

'Oh, really, James. Don't be so ridiculous. He didn't seem like that at all. You've taken a dislike to him and you don't even know him.'

'I haven't,' I replied. 'I'll wait and judge as I find. I didn't take to him ringing up and trying to take the field next door on his first day here I admit.'

'Well, I don't think you'll find him a problem at all,' she stated and walked huffily off to her own office.

I had a sense of foreboding about this Castle, nothing concrete but I vaguely detected trouble. If he thought that Gail would be his ally in the office then we were certainly due for some fireworks. I didn't have time to dwell on the matter as there was an unhappy man hovering in the hall and I was in a tearing hurry to get home. George Pratt was due to have lunch with us at Cordwainers and I didn't want to be late. George was particular about punctuality and giving the right impressions. Unfortunately a coach, full of old ladies from Sidcup, had reversed into the public lavatories in the car park and the resulting confusion had ended up in the estate office.

It wasn't even my problem. The lavatories came under the jurisdiction of the local council, which in my view was the limit of their capabilities, and the accident the domain of the police. However, since the closure of our police station and an absence of any constables in the village, the estate office had become the unofficial place to report any misdemeanours.

'There was a blind spot in me mirror, guv,' the driver was telling me for the umpteenth time. 'I've a bloody good record on the buses, never had so much as a scratch before this.'

'How bad is the damage?' I asked. 'Can't you drive home and sort it out from there?'

'Naw, guv, it's smashed the bloody lights. Can't go back with no lights can I?'

'Well I suppose not.'

'I'll ring me guvnor and he'll have to send up a replacement vehicle to take the old girls home. Mind if I use your phone?'

'Go ahead,' I offered. 'I'll get my secretary to help you out as I've got to dash.'

I left him to make his arrangements whilst I finished dictating a letter for Anne to type.

'There'll be a bus here in about three hours,' he told me. 'I've to stay put and wait for a tow truck.'

'Good, well I'm glad that's dealt with. Ask Anne if you need anything else.'

I raced out to my Land Rover and sped home. George was only staying for an hour or so and I was already ten minutes late. His enormous great Mercedes was in front of the house when I arrived.

'George, how good to see you,' I said, walking into the kitchen. 'Sorry I'm late, you know how it is.'

'Don't worry, Sophie's looking after me,' he boomed and nearly pulled my arm out of its socket as he grabbed my outstretched hand. 'Marvellous to be here. Hope I can have a quick look around after lunch. See what you've got going on farming wise. Poor buggers, I should think you're working your balls off just to break even.'

'Prices aren't good, George, I admit, but it's not quite that bad yet.'

'Tenants at Rumshott are all telling me it is,' he stormed on. 'All wanting a bit knocked off the rent. I keep telling 'em, I can't be too lenient or his lordship'll be down to his last butler!'

I laughed. 'Well, we haven't got any of those here.'

We sat down to lunch. George seemed a bit distracted and was not his usual self. It soon became clear what the reason for his edginess was.

'James,' he said. 'I'm afraid this is not just a social visit.'

'No, George? Is there something I can help you with?'

'There very well might be,' he said between mouthfuls, bits of food occasionally spraying across the table.

'I would be delighted to help you, George, just say what you want.'

'The thing is James, things haven't been working out with your replacement.'

'Oh, really, that's a surprise. She seemed very well qualified,' I offered, wondering where the conversation might be leading.

'She is, she is. Not only well qualified but efficient as well.'

'What's the problem then?'

'The problem is Lady Leghorn. She hates her. She thinks his lordship's taken too much of a shine to her and doesn't like a woman doing the job anyway.'

'Surely you can see off Lady Leghorn, George. You've always managed it in the past.'

'Not this time. She's on the warpath, sabres rattling, armed to the teeth.'

'I see.'

'That's why I am here. I wondered if you would like to have your old job back,' he said bluntly.

I was flabbergasted. Surely George didn't think I would want the job now.

'That's very flattering, George, but my future's here.'

'I've got it all worked out for you, James. We'll give you a pay rise so you'll be getting more than you get here and you'll only have to work four days a week.'

'Even so, it would mean being away from Sophie and the farm at least three nights a week.'

'Nonsense, you could commute. It's only taken me an hour to get down here today.'

I did not need to be reminded of George's driving. I knew that the journey took at least ninety minutes. The offer was deeply flattering though I was glad I was not tempted in the slightest. Perhaps if the offer had come when the only jobs available to me were in estate agency I would have thought about it. But now all I could think about was how happy Sophie and I were at Cordwainers and how much I enjoyed working for Sir Charles. That was my future and George's offer only made me realise how much I valued the life I had now.

Sophie's attention had been distracted and she was peering out the window with consternation.

'George, what's your car doing in the moat?'

'What?'

'Your car. I think it's rolled into the moat.'

He jumped up and rushed to look.

'Bugger it,' he yelled, 'you're right. Quick.'

We all rushed outside. Fortunately his car had settled in about two feet of water on the edge of a shelf before the moat deepened.

'What are you doing, George?' I shouted as he tore off his shoes.

'Got to get it out quickly before water gets into the electrics,' he bellowed back.

'Wait, you'll never move it, it's thick mud. And, no, don't get in there . . .'

It was too late. He was in. Not realising that the moat shelved steeply, he abruptly disappeared from view and reappeared some moments later, covered in pond weed and spluttering profanities.

'What the bloody hell . . .' he spat, 'happened there?'

He clambered out absolutely drenched. 'That is a right buggers' muddle.'

Sophie took him off to get changed and I fetched a tractor to pull the thing out. It wasn't damaged and started as soon as I turned the key. George, however, was looking faintly ridiculous in a dressing gown and a blanket.

There was no time to finish our lunch as George had to get going and I needed to return to the estate office. We said some rather hasty goodbyes and I prayed that George's car did not break down on his way home. None of either Sophie's nor my clothes had the slightest hope of fitting him, so he left clad in the dressing gown carrying a plastic bag of sodden wet belongings.

'I'll have a tour round the farm next time,' he shouted as he reversed. 'It'll be purely social then, I promise!'

'Make sure you bring a spare set of clothes,' Sophie cried as he liberally sprayed us with gravel before speeding off into the distance.

I arrived back at my office to find a queue of old ladies from Sidcup waiting to use the lavatory as the public ones were out of order. In all the excitement at home, I had forgotten the plight of the stricken coach party, which was still waiting for the replacement vehicle. One way or another, it did not seem a good day for travellers.

Chapter 13

I watched Sir Charles' Morris Traveller draw to a shuddering halt outside my office window. He climbed out followed by one of his poodles which, spotting a cat, tore off in pursuit across the market place. A lot of shouting ensued as the dog disappeared down the road.

'Bloody dawg's gorn orf,' he shouted as he came into the office. 'Damn thing's after a cat.'

He didn't seem very perturbed. I would have been worried that it might get run over.

'I can't stop long,' he said, 'I'm in a frightful hurry. Ring Hole and get him to pop down and fetch her would you? He can take her back to the Hall, wretched thing.'

'Yes, of course, Sir Charles.'

There was the inevitable delay as the telephone rang and rang as Hole presumably hurried along the passages from the depths of the house. I did not imagine that he'd be overjoyed at the prospect of fetching the dog.

Apart from intruding on his other duties the only means of conveying himself down to the village was on his ancient bicycle. This wasn't wholly due to Sir Charles' stringent motor policy but also due to the fact that Hole couldn't really drive. It was always a touch and go matter when he was asked to take Sir Charles' car to the front door of the house. Many times I had seen it lurch awkwardly across the gravel sweep with Hole grimly hanging on to the steering wheel.

He arrived rather breathless on the telephone.

'Frampton Hall,' he answered.

'James Aden here, Mr Hole. I'm afraid Sir Charles has lost one of his dogs. He wonders if you'd be kind enough to find it as he's got to rush off somewhere.'

'Very good, Mr Aden,' he replied without a trace of rancour in his voice. 'Do we have any idea where the animal might be found?'

'Last seen disappearing down Market Lane in pursuit of a cat,' I explained. 'I'm afraid that's all I know.'

Sir Charles was pacing impatiently around my office.

'Must get on,' he announced as I rang off. 'The point of calling in is this. An urgent problem has arisen at the Hall. There's a frightful pong coming from behind the panelling in the library. I can hardly sit in there. Could you get someone to sort it out? I've got the Poodle Association Dinner here on Friday and I like to take them in there after we've eaten.'

Not relishing the interruption I drove up to the Hall. There was, as Sir Charles said, a dreadful smell in the library and I suspected a rat had died within the wall cavity. Frankly there was nothing we could do bar dismantling the panelling so the poodle people would have to use a different room.

I worked in the office for the remainder of the day prioritising the most urgent matters, until I was interrupted by the roar of a powerful motor car arriving in the square. A brand-new red Ferrari, it stopped and lay still, quivering with testosterone-fuelled menace. A casually dressed young man climbed out, accompanied by a stick-thin leggy blonde. Both of them had sunglasses pushed back over their hair in a fashionable Riviera pose. Castle, I assumed. This was confirmed by an excited squeal from upstairs as Gail rushed over to the window.

I turned back to my papers and dictated a short letter to the local secretary of the Frampton Ferret club giving them permission to hold their biannual ferrets convention, as they called it, on the estate. The story of Mr Thwaite, their secretary, attending last year's summer fete distracted me for a moment. In a desperate move to attract more spectators to his display he had put a ferret down his trousers to prove what likeable little creatures they were. Unsurprisingly, the poor creature had bitten something it shouldn't have. I understood that Mr Thwaite's antics had caused some swelling, but sadly not of spectator numbers.

There was another squeal from upstairs followed by Gail's heavy descent down the stairs and I heard the estate office door open.

'I wondered if James Aden was in,' a drawling voice enquired.

'He is, but very tied up at the moment,' Anne replied. 'Can I say who it is?'

The man was interrupted by Gail landing in the reception hall.

'Hello, Trevor,' she gushed breathlessly. 'I have just come down to make some coffee. Would you like some?'

I doubt he had ever seen anyone so excited by the thought of making a cup of coffee, but he gave Gail a full blast of his charm.

'I'm all right, thanks. Just thought I'd come and introduce myself to the big cheese here,' he drawled.

'James you mean? Of course, I'm sure he's about.'

Anne interrupted. 'Gail, he's busy. He's asked not to be disturbed.'

'Oh, has he?' she said. 'Isn't it worth asking, seeing as Mr Castle has taken the trouble to call in?'

'It's no trouble,' he said, 'I was just passing.'

'I saw your car,' continued Gail, 'it's lovely.'

'Thank you. We had better be going. I'll call in again some other time.'

'I think that would be better,' agreed Anne.

'Sure thing, and see you about, eh, Gail,' he said, slamming the door as he left.

The raptures that she went into made me squirm behind my closed door. Certainly, Castle didn't seem put out by it. I wondered if Gail had seen the tough competition draped over the bonnet of the Ferrari outside. Castle obviously liked having women throw themselves at him. As he returned to his car I noticed that he was wearing tight black leather trousers. I was certain that he would soon be the centre of village gossip as there was no way Frampton was ready for the sight of men in leather trousers.

He creaked across the square and to my interest I saw Isobel heading his way. I wondered what he'd make of her and watched as Castle spotted her and changed course as though to intercept her. For a brief moment the medieval market place took on the appearance of a Western movie set. The girl by the car was eyeing Isobel dangerously, I was held motionless in the saloon bar arid the heroine hovered hesitantly as the sharp shooter blocked her path.

The moment was broken by the arrival of the fresh fish van from Lowestoft making its weekly visit. Despite it parking in my eyeline I could just see Castle attempting to engage Isobel in conversation. I was amused to see that she gave him short shrift, walking away at great pace after they had only exchanged a few words.

Chapter 14

I looked in dismay at a pile of post and dozens of telephone messages to deal with and decided that a whole day in the estate office was necessary to try and get through it.

One letter was an application to rent an empty shop in the High Street. It caught my eye because it appeared to be more interesting than the usual requests. The village was awash with gift, craft and brie a brae shops which were so popular with the tourists. This letter referred to a possible art gallery exhibiting the work of local artists. Sir Charles had recently said that he thought that there were too many gift shops and wanted some new ideas.

It never failed to amaze me what visitors to the village would buy but the success of the gift shops defied my belief. I would have thought that some local pottery or perhaps a sketch of the market place would be ideal. Or a hand-knitted sweater made from Suffolk wool, even a jar of local honey. No. It seemed they wanted a plastic model of Big Ben, made in Korea, a policeman in a glass ball who got snowed on when shaken, or a china donkey straddled by a Spanish peasant.

Predominantly our visitors were British followed closely by Americans and Japanese. The Japanese were obviously identifiable by their looks but another defining characteristic was that they always stuck together in large groups. Busily they would tear around the village taking video films and then rush back to their coach. They seemed to live in fear of being left behind. The British and Americans did things in a more leisurely style, licking ice creams that dripped on to their shoes, taking the occasional photograph and wandering through the shops. Of course the Americans wore hideous clothes: checked trousers and baseball caps for the men, shapeless slacks and training shoes for the women. The British were more complicated. The older generation were usually fairly smartly dressed. Elderly gentlemen in tweed jackets and ties would sit in the baking sunshine with never a thought of undoing a top button. Their wives, with dresses matching their handbags, would peer intently at the surroundings and then sit and wait for their bus. The younger British had started dressing a bit like the Americans but without the garish clashes that clearly originated on the far side of the Atlantic.

Anyway, I thought that Sir Charles would be keen on this gallery proposal so I put the letter aside for his comments and began a mammoth session on the paperwork. By the time I had finished it was nearly dusk but the sunset was so spectacular I decided to set off on an early evening walk around the village before heading for home.

I came across Miss Smithson watering some flower tubs outside her cottage. They were full of bright red geraniums. I hadn't seen her since the handbag incident which had now been fully resolved.

'Good evening, Miss Smithson,' I said, making her start.

She looked up. 'Oh, it's you, Mr Aden,' she shouted. 'a lovely evening, isn't it?'

'Indeed,' I agreed, 'just off for a walk to make the most of it.'

'I wish I could do the same,' she continued. 'In my younger days I spent many such times doing just that. It's too much for me now though. A bit of pottering around here is the limit I'm afraid.'

I commiserated long enough to be polite but I didn't want to get involved in a lengthy discussion about her ailments. Two topics I had discovered were enough to pass an entire lifetime of idle conversation in the village. Health and weather. And it was so easy. All one needed to say was, 'How are you?' or 'Lovely day,' emit some 'oh dears' and grunts of agreement at regular, and not necessarily appropriate intervals, and twenty minutes soon passed by.

Early evening was a busy time in the village. People had returned from work and were now either in their gardens or out with their dogs. The retired folk had finished tea and were eager to embark upon the next session of village news. It was similar to a television soap opera except that it was possible to take part.

Just along the road from Miss Smithson, I met Tony and Valerie Taylor accompanied by their grossly overweight Labrador, Sandy. I knew them as we had met at one or two cocktail parties. The Taylors lived in a lovely seventeenth century house that had once been an inn. Everyone referred to it as the Old Cock but when the Taylors had bought it they had renamed it Toval House. They were those sort of people. Actually it was number 43 Brett Street but I suppose, as an accountant, he liked to get away from numbers at home.

They were in the gin and tonic set which fitted somewhere between the Buckley social strata and the majority of the village. Tony was a partner in a firm in town, played golf and sat on the parish council. His wife read magazines about Agas, was a member of the Women's Institute and spent her time following the advice of one or the other. They were a well-meaning couple and much involved with village activities but I found them hard work. They seemed to want to socialise in Sir Charles' circle but had no idea that he would have considered their lifestyle beyond the pale. He'd be more likely to read a porn magazine than *Aga Week* and wouldn't be seen dead on a golf course, a game he thought was played by building society managers and people who owned garages.

'Ah, good evening, James,' said Tony. 'How's everything on the western front?'

The Taylors were strong on joviality and euphemisms. For a moment I thought they meant the west front of the Hall.

'You know, the estate and Sir Charles?' he prompted.

'Oh, I see,' I caught on. 'All fine, I think, thank you. And you? Both looking well, I see.'

'Top form old boy,' replied Tony. 'Lovely evening. Thought we'd take a stroll, see what's going on. By the way, I suppose you know a new chap has moved into the Old Rectory?'

'Yes, of course,' I said.

'We've been told,' whispered Valerie, 'that the new owner is a film producer. Made an awful lot of money out of, erm, what do you call them, Tony?'

'Blue movies.'

'Ssh dear, don't say things like that so loudly. Not in public.'

I must have looked surprised at this information because she then added, 'You know, dirty films.'

'Oh, really,' I said. 'Who on earth told you that?'

'Well, I can't say,' she continued, 'but what I do know is that there's been a succession of attractive young girls in and out of there ever since he arrived. I shouldn't be surprised if they're making a film at this moment.'

'I think I'll have to go up and have a look for myself,' said Tony, with a wink of an eye.

'Don't you dare,' his wife started, rising to the bait.

'Anyway, we don't know that, darling. Better not start saying things like this until we know. Do you know, James?'

'I've heard the man's in the computer business.'

'Oh, they all say that,' Valerie went on. 'Computers covers anything nowadays.'

'I'm sure it will become clear in due course. You'll have to invite the chap to one of your drinks parties,' I joked.

The wonder of village gossip. I laughed to myself. Newcomers were always the topic of conversation and we'd had some incredibly inaccurate tales in the past although we'd never had a porn king before. But this was interesting. I had disliked Castle from the moment I met him and now I reasoned that perhaps this was because my sixth sense had picked up something about him. The implications could be serious. The scandal of having a pornographer on the estate would cause great distress to Sir Charles. I would have to try to do a bit of digging into Castle's past.

As I headed away from the village I hoped that I would not meet anyone else. I wanted some peace and quiet to enjoy the countryside and my own thoughts without interruption. Much as I loved the village life, the inconsequential mutterings, the fact that most people knew one another and what they were doing I wanted to be on my own.

Luck was on my side and I continued undisturbed along the lane turning off on to a disused railway track that cut across the estate. The branch railway and station had long since gone, a casualty of Dr Beeching's rationalisation in the 1960s. It was a great pity as a local station would have been of benefit, the nearest now being ten miles away. Even that was a branch line taking a further half an hour to reach the main London line. When the railways had been constructed in the nineteenth century many of the great landed estates benefited from the easier access to London and the provincial towns. In due course it became customary for those landowners with estates in Scotland to travel there by rail, accompanied by their entourage of servants, dogs and all the paraphernalia needed for a month's sport in the Highlands. They could cover the long journey with the comfort of a dining car and sleeping quarters. Some landowners, including the Buckleys, had given their permission for the railways to cross their land subject to certain conditions. There was a story about one such peer, an elderly earl, who had demanded that a private station should be built for his sole use. It duly was and the earl used the railway to get to his estate in Scotland. Having spent the night on the train he was approached by one of the guards the following morning and cautioned that some fellow passengers had been woken by his lordship's dogs barking in the night. Furiously the earl had replied that if there were any more complaints from members of the public, he would close his station!

I walked on, delighting in the freedom of the countryside and taking pleasure in the intricacies of nature. The lush green growth of summer, a multitude of colourful wild flowers and the calls of birds perched in the trees combined to improve my mood. I left the track and set off along a path across a wheat field, the ears beginning to ripen and turn gold, swaying slightly in a light breeze. Sky larks sang high above, so high that they couldn't be seen, their ceaseless song the only sound. I was thankful for the career I had chosen; it had provided a job that enabled me to be so close to all of this. I climbed towards the crest of the field, the clear open expanse of the East Anglian landscape falling away beyond. From this point I could just make out the dark mass of a wood over at Cordwainers and I wondered what Sophie was up to. It was a shame that she wasn't here to enjoy the walk with me but she tended to keep out of the estate life, believing that otherwise we would become too immersed in it all.

When I returned to my office in the square, it wasn't long before I heard some clattering in the street and I recognised Mr Parson's voice.

'You've got one of those things now, have you?' he said, his strident tones carried through the evening light.

'Yes,' a voice replied, 'absolutely marvellous machine. Can't think how we ever did without them.'

'Oh, has Barbara got one as well?' Mr Parsons wanted to know.

I didn't dare look out for fear of getting drawn into the conversation but I could see him, smartly dressed and leaning on a walking stick.

'Indeed. One each, you see. Means we can go off round the village together.'

I realised their discussion centred around the merits of an electric wheelchair, a profusion of which had recently sprouted amongst the better off villagers. They were more like a golf buggy than a wheelchair although their purpose was the same. It wouldn't be long before another topic was added to my enquiries about health and weather. Wheelchairs.

Chapter 15

'What's that bloody awful smell?' commented Sir Charles as he walked into the estate office the following morning.

'Ah,' I said hesitantly. 'It's, um,' I dropped my voice to a whisper, 'it's Gail's latest perfume. A bit industrial, isn't it?'

'Good God. Smells like lavatory cleaner. Is she washing herself in it?'

'Well, I don't know what she does with it. The trouble is she's after another bloke, I think. That's what a new smell usually means.'

'I should leave the door open if I were you,' Sir Charles suggested. 'I imagine it doesn't pong in your office, let's go in there.'

I had noticed that recently Gail's hair had become blonder, the tan darker and her cleavage deeper. I had noticed these things because I saw her every day but even a complete stranger would have assumed the smell was unusual.

'Thought she was having it orf with one of the grooms,' said Sir Charles.

'No, if you remember, I mentioned I thought that was over. She's set her sights on someone else.'

'Extraordinary woman that,' remarked the baronet. 'Seems to have an enormous appetite for men!'

'Yes, it's rather a dramatic lifestyle. Not very settling, as we can vouch for in here. Always some upheaval.'

'It's no wonder her poor husband ran orf. Now the thing is I saw the Brigadier the other day and he wants to see you. About the gymkhana. Having it the Bank Holiday Monday after the carnival. As far as I'm concerned they can use the park as usual. Can you sort it out with him?'

He hadn't been gone long when Anne put a call through.

'Brigadier Hand for you, James.'

'Thanks, Anne. Hallo, James Aden speaking,' I said.

'Brigadier Hand here,' he barked down the phone.

'Morning, Brigadier.'

'Morning, Aden. How are you keeping? Good . . . what?' he carried on shouting.

Brigadier Augustus Hand, retired, ex-Royal Artillery, normally organised the Frampton Hunter Trials, for which he'd already collared me to assist, but was also the district commissioner of the local branch of the Pony Club and organiser of their annual gymkhana. He was an extremely efficient man, used to commanding his troops, and had all the young mothers running around as though he was deploying soldiers behind enemy lines. Despite his fore-boding presence he was a likeable man although his deafness was a minor distraction. He rarely used his hearing aid and had explained rather bluntly, when I'd first met him, why he couldn't hear.

'Hallo, I'm James Aden,' I had introduced myself.

'What's that?' he shouted 'Can't hear you.'

'James Aden,' I shouted back.

'You haven't shaven. Strange thing to say.'

'No, my name's Aden,' I tried again.

'A maiden, huh, not married? Ah, well, plenty of time for that,' he continued. 'Shouldn't worry, you're a young man. Didn't get married meself till I was forty. Too busy shooting huns. That's why I'm deaf.'

Our conversation today was equally hampered by similar misunderstandings.

'Saw Sir Charles the other day. Said everything was in order for us to use the park,' he said. 'Just liaise with you over the details.'

'Yes, I've just seen him this morning,' I replied. 'We'll have the grass mown by the end of the month and move the cattle out the weekend before. Does that give you enough time to get everything ready?'

'What? If you'd be good enough to get the grass mown and the cattle out say a week before, that would give us enough time to get the place ready.'

'Yes, we'll do that,' I shouted.

'Excellent, Aden,' he bellowed, 'knew I could count on you.'

'That's perfectly all right, Brigadier,' I bellowed back. 'Will you want to use the lavatories in the stable block this year?'

'Teas in the stable block? No, we've never had teas in the stable block. We 'ave 'em in a marquee.'

I tried another tack. 'Will you be hiring loos?'

'I shouldn't think so,' he retorted, chuckling. 'We've never had 'em before.'

'The file says you did two years ago, Brigadier.'

'No. We've never had queues as far as I can remember.'

'No, Brigadier. I said loos not queues. I gather last year they used the ones in the stables, but before that you hired them. Loos,' I shouted, 'toilets.'

'Ah, yes. Now last year we used the ones in the stable block but they're a bit far away so this year we're going to hire some. We did it once before you know.'

'So I understand, Brigadier. The sort that look like blue telephone kiosks.'

There was a brief silence. 'Can't think why we'd need a telephone kiosk,' he said.

'I said the loos look like a telephone kiosk.'

'We'll hire the loos but do without the phone,' he assured me. 'That all right with you, what?'

'That's fine. I never suggested hiring a phone. If it's that desperate they can always use the one in the High Street.'

'I didn't know there were any in the High Street,' he continued.

'Any what?' I yelled.

'Lavatories.'

'No, there aren't, Brigadier. There's a phone box.'

'Good God, man. They can't go in there,' he exclaimed, entirely missing the point. 'It's illegal.'

It was easier to discuss things with Brigadier Hand face to face. There seemed to be less chance of a misunderstanding. We arranged to meet the week before the event to iron out any last-minute problems.

The telephone rang again as soon as I'd put it down.

'Dennis Catchpole on the line for you,' said Anne. 'Do you want to speak to him?'

'Ah, yes, thanks Anne, He's ringing about the tractor for the cricket club.'

'Dennis,' I said.

'Morning, James,' he chirped. 'How's tricks?'

'Fine thanks. I hope you're ringing about this tractor.'

'That's right, boy,' he confirmed in his broad East Anglian dialect.

He was an unusual man in as much as that no one knew what means he lived on. At one time he had kept a lot of pigs but failing eyesight had necessitated the scaling down of this enterprise. In his early fifties the best guess seemed to be that he had planned his pension wisely and taken early retirement. Suffolk born and bred he knew everyone and spent his days wandering around the place helping people. He would do anything despite his near blindness, his only concession to his hardship was that he walked with a stick. It was not a white one but a long, horn-handled shepherd's crook, which he waved wildly in front of him as though he was scything a field of nettles.

He was considered to be a knowledgeable tractor mechanic and it was in this capacity that I had engaged his assistance to find an old tractor to pull the mower up at the cricket ground. The previous one had been stolen and I had given up any hope of the police finding it when the local sergeant, filling in some report form, had asked me whether it was left- or right-hand drive. So I had asked Dennis to find a suitable replacement and he'd come up with an old grey Fergie, a little 1950s tractor ideal for the job.

'I'm going with the brother-in-law to fetch it this morning,' he told me. 'I reckon you want to meet me at the cricket ground about midday, boy.'

'Okay. What about some money? You'll need to pay for it.'

'Naw, that'll be all right,' he said. 'The gaffer selling it says as it's for Sir Charles you can send 'im a cheque. £500 it'll be and £25 for the brother-in-law's lorry.'

'Thanks, Dennis, that's great. I'll see you at twelve.'

He was a man of action. If he said he'd do something he'd do it, with a resolute disregard for his limited eyesight.

When I found him at the cricket ground, true to form, having handled the whole issue from start to finish he had decided to offload the tractor himself. A large man, topped with a filthy pork pie hat, he was sitting astride the little tractor balanced on two planks of wood positioned at the back of the lorry.

There was a heated discussion in place between the two men.

'You've gorn and got the bloody thing askew again Dennis,' cried the brother-in-law.

'It's no good shouting at me, boy. Am I over t'left or right?'

'You're about to fall off to the left.'

'Is that the left as I'm coming down or as I face t'wagon?'

'As you face t'wagon.'

Dennis started to turn the steering wheel.

'Don't do that,' shouted the brother-in-law. 'You'll have the bloody front wheels orf.'

'I'll go up and start agin then,' Dennis decided. He inched the tractor slowly forwards.

'Tell me if I'm straight yet,' he asked.

'Bit more, bit more. That'll do yer.'

'I'll 'ave another go then, this time tell me afore I go awry, will yer, Brian.'

'Yup. You keep her straight, Dennis.'

He started the next attempt and slowly backed the machine down the planks. Anybody else would have wondered why he was attempting to negotiate such a job but if you knew Dennis you'd also know that to suggest anything else would be met with hoots of derision. I kept silent and held my breath.

'You're getting the hang of it now, Dennis,' shouted Brian helpfully. 'You're about halfway.'

'What you saying, boy?' replied Dennis, losing concentration.

'I said you're about . . . stop, stop,' he shrieked. 'You're coming orf the bloody side agin.'

Unfortunately he'd left the warning too late. There was a terrible moment when time seemed to stand still with the tractor poised in midair as it left the planks. Then, faster than Dennis had intended, it reached the springy turf of the outfield. The tractor bounced up and down as it landed heavily on its tyres. Dennis, bouncing with it, hung on grimly to the steering wheel, his hat poised at a rakish angle. When everything had settled and appeared to be in one piece Dennis spoke.

'Just as well t'club captain ain't 'ere. After all,' he said slightly misquoting, 'when the eye don't see, the heart won't grieveth.'

Chapter 16

As I drove up the High Street one lunchtime, cutting a swathe through the groups of tourists idly wandering in the street, I recognised a group of students whom we employed as casual labour loitering outside the King's Head pub. Apart from all the usual farming enterprises there was an area devoted to growing strawberries and students looking for holiday work came and picked the fruit which was then packed and sent off to the London markets. I suspected that this would be our final year in the fruit business as it was becoming less and less profitable each season. The increasing burden of European bureaucracy was threatening its existence. It frustrated me how our own politicians, with no more spine to them than a soggy vol au vent could allow this to happen. The laws had become totally bizarre. The pickers for instance, who put the fruit into plastic containers out in the field, dressed as they pleased and I daresay had a pee in the hedge if the need arose, then carried on picking without washing their hands. The Europeans were very happy about this. However the ladies in the pack house, who merely put the lids on the containers, had to wear a hat. There seemed nothing we could do. European directives bombarded us on every issue, from farm waste control to minimum pay, the shape of a carrot to the ingredients of home-made jam. It wouldn't be long before we had a statutory size for the length of a bull's penis. The idiots in Westminster were as much use as an ashtray on a motor cycle.

I arrived at the office to find it looking decidedly messy. Usually, squint-eyed Dolly kept the place clean, coming in once a week; but she'd gone off for a fortnight's holiday in Lowestoft. Her absence gave me some peace as she was likely to chatter inexhaustibly whenever I saw her. Initially she used to come in after we had left for the night and it had slightly concerned me that she might find some confidential papers lying around and start gossiping. She loved to know exactly what was going on and by some extraordinary perceptive means picked up details that convinced me she had the hearing capabilities of a bat. So when her daughter had started working nightshifts in a chicken-packing factory and Dolly had to stay in to look after her grandchildren, we gladly agreed she could clean during the day. If it was safer, it was a great deal more irritating. She didn't appear to notice that we were also trying to get on with our work. She joined in. The week before she'd gone to Lowestoft she had involved herself in some negotiations over renovating a collection of paintings up at the Hall.

'I believe Sir Charles would like the work to be done before the autumn,' I had said to Mr Turnbull-Harrington on the telephone. Mr Turnbull-Harrington of Turnbull-Harrington, Fitzgerald and Co., Fine Art Specialists of Dover Street, London W1, was the senior partner of a highly respectable firm noted for its connections with the aristocracy.

'Here's a nice cup o' tea for you, my love,' Dolly bustled in, banging the tray down on my desk. 'Autumn'll soon be upon us,' she remarked, 'it'll be early if I know anything about it. Them tits what was in my garden 'ave gorn already.'

'Absolutely no problem whatsoever, sir,' replied the

smooth, cultivated tones of Turnbull-Harrington. 'We shall need to remove the paintings within the next fortnight.'

'Surprising how quickly the leaves'll begin to turn,' continued Dolly.

I gesticulated at her that I would prefer to be left alone but she misconstrued my actions and, taking a duster out of her apron, set to work on some bookshelves.

'That would be excellent,' I said. 'I know Sir Charles will be pleased. They've had some of these family portraits since about 1640, I believe, some of the most important in the house.'

'Ooh, they have had 'em a long time,' remarked Dolly. 'I always tell my Gordon I don't like stuff hanging around too long. We like to change our pictures round a bit, we do. Get bored looking at the same old thing.'

'Absolutely,' said Mr Turnbull-Harrington, oblivious to the duster. 'Some of Rembrandt's first work completed during his so-called "third Amsterdam period".'

'Usually take 'em to a car boot sale,' Dolly told me. 'Always get a few quid especially if the glass ain't broken.'

'I'll need to notify the insurers that the paintings are leaving the house,' I informed the art dealer.

'I love 'im dearly, my Gordon, but he can be a clumsy oaf,' she explained. 'Last time we went to the sale, he broke two of 'em. Had to let 'em go for a fiver at end of the day.'

'Do you have the insurance valuation to hand, Mr Aden?' asked Turnbull-Harrington.

'Yes, it's here in front of me,' I said. 'As a group, Christies have put a value of £80.5 million.'

'Lost me ten quid that broken glass did. And when you think it cost seven to have a pitch you begin to wonder whether it's worth the bother.' Dolly had her back to my increasingly frantic gestures.

'That doesn't surprise me at all,' agreed the expert. 'Stunning examples of that period and I have to say we are extremely excited, indeed honoured to be undertaking this work for Sir Charles.'

'Our insurers will obviously need to talk to your own. No doubt they arrange some sort of joint responsibility whilst they're in your care. I'll get ours to give you a call. The man we deal with is called James Carruthers,' I explained to him.

'I know a Jim Carruthers,' piped up Dolly from the bookcase. 'Ooh, brings back terrible memories does that name.'

'I'll expect his call then,' said Turnbull-Harrington.

'Kept a lot of pigs over at Round Hill,' she went on.

'You'll find him extremely helpful,' I told him.

'Ever such a nice man he was. Always had a bit of time for everyone. He'd stop in t'street for a word, however much of a hurry he was in. Smelt of pigs, I 'ave to say, but you couldn't hold that against 'im, it were his trade.'

'Well, Mr Aden, no doubt we'll speak again soon. In fact once I've spoken to Mr Carruthers I'll arrange a moving date. Rest assured that we will take every precaution with these masterpieces.'

'I'm sure you will, Mr Turnbull-Harrington, neither of us want any calamities.'

'It were a terrible calamity,' agreed Dolly. 'Fell into his own slurry pit he did. Drowned . . . awful way to go, dying in pig muck.'

'Dolly!' I barked as soon as I'd put the phone down. 'Could you leave this office until later please. I'm going out in an hour and need some peace until then.'

I went out an hour later to meet the members of the Frampton Carnival committee to discuss the final details of this year's event. It was a part of my job to sit as the estate's representative on many village committees, in the main merely to offer some help to the actual running of any events. Wherever possible I avoided the endless discussions of committee meetings where deliberation over the most trivial of matters could rouse members into a ferocious zeal.

I arrived a little bit late to find a heated argument in force concerning sausages. The chairman of the Carnival committee, a small, well-intentioned man who spent much of the year bustling about the village, was vainly trying to prevent war breaking out over the catering arrangements.

'We have always had De Vere's Sausages,' bellowed Daphne Frobisher. 'I can't remember a carnival without them.'

'I know,' replied a very red-faced Mrs Joyce, 'but this hog roast is far superior. Proper joints of pork, sliced in front of you. It's better value and better quality . . .'

'De Vere's Sausages are the best quality I've ever tasted,' interrupted Mrs Frobisher.

'Please, let me finish, Daphne,' said Mrs Joyce stiffly. 'What you seem to forget is that one never knows what's inside a sausage. They might be quality as you say, but quality what? Eh? What's in those sausages? Could be all sorts of additives for all we know.'

'Utter nonsense,' barked Mrs Frobisher. 'It's good wholesome food.'

'The other's 100 per cent meat, much more wholesome I would have thought. We don't want E numbers and stuff like that. Makes the children hyperactive.'

'My children have never had a problem with De Vere's Sausages.'

'Well, mine have never had a problem with a hog roast,' retorted Mrs Joyce.

'I don't think you should have changed what we've always done without consulting the committee,' declared Mrs Frobisher, looking at her chairman for support.

'I was put in charge of catering,' snorted Mrs Joyce, clearly wishing she hadn't. 'If I'd known there was going to be all this fuss I'd never have volunteered.'

'Ladies, ladies, I really think it's too late to change anything now,' interjected Paul Flower, the chairman. 'Personally I don't think it matters which we have. Why don't we see how it goes this year and then discuss it again before the next carnival.'

'What about vegetarians?' asked a miffed Mrs Frobisher. 'De Vere's did vegetarian sausages, as well you know. Lots of people don't eat meat.'

'They'll be able to get cheese sandwiches from the WI tent.'

'A lot of them don't eat cheese either.'

This abrupt reminder of why I avoided committees like the plague sank home. 'Excuse me for butting in,' I announced loudly to the collective gathering, 'but I can only stay for half an hour and I need to know what the farm men have got to do to get the field ready. It's been mown and I imagine you'll want a load of straw bales for the ringside seats, a couple of tractors in case vehicles get stuck, what else?'

The sausages were forgotten although I had no doubt the debate would rage on again later. Daphne Frobisher was known for her stubbornness and usually won her arguments by beating her opponents into submission through boredom. I scribbled down a list of jobs that the estate had to undertake and promised Mr Flower my help on the day.

Chapter 17

I woke early on Thursday morning with the sun filtering through the curtains and the sound of birdsong loud outside the open window. I loved our bedroom with its oak timbers and whitewashed plaster walls. Half the space was taken up by a four-poster bed, luxuriously comfortable and welcoming with its pale blue and gold silk drapes. It was the haven where Sophie and I could hide away from the bustle of the farm and estate life.

I got up and leant out through the bay window. A clear night had given way to a fresh day. Bright blue sky with not a cloud in sight. I gazed over the well-kept gardens that surrounded the house and watched some ducks swimming on the moat which divided the lawns from the paddock. Beyond, climbing the other side of the small valley, the open countryside was turning a pale gold as the barley began to ripen.

'Sophie,' I turned and looked at her lying in bed, 'how about going out tonight? We haven't been out for ages, have we?'

She sat up yawning, her long dark hair tousled over the pillows.

'Um, that'd be nice. Where shall we go?'

'Let's have dinner at the Horseshoes. I'll book a table. If it's still warm we can eat by the river. Will you be back in time?'

'Oh, yes, I hope to be home by mid-afternoon.'

Sophie was planning on driving up to Norwich to buy some material for new dining room curtains. Gradually the house was changing as she put her mark on its style, the rather plain uninspired feel of a bachelor's being replaced by a livelier, more colourful design. I had a day at the office to get through which began with a brusque telephone call from Sir Charles.

'Morning, James,' he started. 'I've a couple of interesting developments here. Firstly, Sebastian rang last night. He's coming for luncheon on Sunday with a lady friend. Didn't think I'd heard him right till he repeated it. Secondly, I had a call from Inglenook, asking if I'd host the Country Landowners' Association dinner here. The big national thing they do.'

'I see,' I said. 'What did you say?'

'To who?'

'Well, both of them, I suppose.'

'Pleased about Sebastian of course, not so about this wretched dinner thing.'

'I can understand that,' I agreed, knowing Sir Charles' dislike of hordes of people in the house.

'Actually, had a bit of a row with old Inglenook about it. I don't mind the CLA, you know quite a useful bunch in their way, but they've invited the Prime Minister. So I told him they could have the dinner here provided no politicians are invited. Especially the PM. Can't stand the bugger as you know. Don't; see why I should entertain him in my house.'

'No, I agree,' I said. 'I'm well aware of your feelings about the present government Sir Charles. Presumably the CLA won't be coming then?'

'Well of course, Inglenook says my pigheadedness has put him in a damned difficult position. Says it would be extremely bad form, if not impossible, to withdraw the invitation to the Prime Minister.'

'I suppose it would,' I mused. 'Might be a good thing though.'

'That's what I said to him. Let the PM know there's still some of us chaps left who can see what he's up to. Trying to turn us into a nation of pansies ruled by a load of weirdos from abroad. Told Inglenook to pass the message on but of course he won't.'

'So it's highly unlikely they'll be having the dinner here then?'

'Unless they change their minds. Now, more importantly, the Carnival on Saturday. What time have I got to open the thing?'

'Officially at two o'clock, Sir Charles. But the procession leaves the Square at one-thirty, arriving at the playing field just before two.'

'Jolly good. I'll meet you and the organiser fellow at one forty-five on the field. See you on Saturday.' With that he was gone.

There was a relaxed holiday feeling about the day helped by the village filling up with tourists staying for the carnival weekend. I felt restless and excited and wanted to get out of the office on such a beautiful day so I rang the groom and asked her to leave a horse ready for me to ride. I decided to go and have a look around the woods and see how Messrs Wright, Coke and Co.'s woodland management programme was progressing.

I drove up to the stables and found Neptune had been left for me. He was a super horse, a seventeen-hand grey gelding, well schooled and with a long comfortable stride. He could be an exciting handful and Sir Charles found him a bit strong nowadays and his tendency to spook at the slightest noise irritating. I liked his liveliness and let him have his head as we cantered across the park. The centuries-old springy turf was perfect for a galloping horse and we cut a route along the bottom of the valley, skirting the great clumps of ancient gnarled oaks that majestically dominated the parkland.

I pulled Neptune to a halt by the lake to admire the view. The water was clear and almost totally still in the heat of the day, the wide shimmering expanse framed at the far end by a columnar stone bridge over which the formal approach to the Hall passed. The imposing south front of the house stood guardian over the landscape and I reflected in awe that all this had remained unchanged for generations.

The thought made me wonder about Sebastian and his forthcoming visit on Sunday. He was such an unusual person that it would take a special type of woman to find him attractive. No doubt his wealth, although he kept that inconspicuous to say the least, would appeal to many but he was wise enough not to be drawn along those lines. He needed to find someone though. It seemed such a terrible waste for all that lay in front of me to pass to a distant relative who may have no real sense of the family's relationship with the land. Sir Charles was increasingly worried about it and was desperate for Sebastian to do something.

I moved on, heading for a gate in the park wall that led into the woodland. The grassy track was overgrown with the dense summer foliage casting a welcome shade from the heat of the sun. We picked our way through, Neptune occasionally shying from a bird that would suddenly fly out of a bush. The scent of the woodland flowers mingled with that of the horse, a combination evocative of many such rides over the estate.

The woods were undisturbed and I found my way to one

of my special places on the whole estate. A small clearing on the brow of a hill from where one could see, in all its glory, the rolling acres of parkland, the reflections of the lake and the Hall a mere blot in the distance. Way beyond, the open undulating countryside of East Anglia stretched towards the horizon. One day perhaps, I might bring Sophie up here for a picnic. A hidden, secret dell that couldn't fail to seduce her.

Eventually I found the foresters working in a far corner of the plantation, the noise of their chainsaws shattering the peace. They stopped when they saw me and we discussed their progress. The area ravaged by storms was beginning to look better, with some sort of order now being extracted from the chaos. Great stacks of timber were piled in neat rows alongside the track ready to be carted off to the sawmill.

Reluctantly I returned to the stables. I couldn't stay out all day and I had letters to write and telephone calls to make. Gail was in the reception hall looking flushed when I walked in.

'Oh, you've just missed Trevor again,' she said.

'Oh, what did he want?'

'He was hoping to catch you.'

'What about?'

'I'm not sure but I think it's about the field,' she explained.

'Why doesn't he make an appointment like everyone else?' I asked her irritably. I didn't like the way she fussed around him so obviously and wondered briefly how far her intended friendship had got.

'Well, he's so busy he's never sure when he can get here,' she told me.

'That's tough then. Most people can make an appointment, however busy they are,' I retorted and went into my office.

As I sat at my desk I thought back to my conversation with Tony and Valerie. I went to Gail's office.

'Listen, Gail,' I said, 'a friendly piece of advice. I think you had better not get too close to Castle.'

'Why would I want to do that?' replied Gail, frostily. 'And even if I did, it would be no business of yours, would it?'

Oh, well. I had tried to warn her.

After the wholesome aroma of country air and horse, Gail's pong of industrial perfume seemed worse that ever.

Anne came in. 'Lover boy called, as you probably gathered,' she said, nodding her head in Gail's direction.

'I've made an appointment for him to see you next week. Is that okay?'

'Yes, that's fine. I've got to see him at some time or other I suppose.'

'I haven't told Gail, otherwise she'd be lying in wait for him,' she added.

I laughed. 'I'm sure she would,' I said, agreeing with her. 'She's not very subtle in her approach, is she?'

'Good heavens, no!' exclaimed Anne. 'She might just as well run into the square naked and throw herself at him.'

'Perish the thought,' I said, imagining her pendulous breasts swinging awkwardly as she streaked across the medieval marketplace. The thought made me think again about Tony and Valerie's words and I resolved to try and do something about it before Gail made a fool of herself.

I concentrated on ploughing through the pile of mundane paperwork that had accumulated. There were requests for cottage repairs, houses to let and a farm review to settle. The draft lease of the shop we were letting as a local art gallery was ready and needed checking. Amongst the pile was an unusual letter from a rose-grower asking for permission to name a new variety he'd bred after Sir Charles' family. There were bills to verify including one for a set of snow chains for Sir Charles' car. Obviously he had no intention of updating it yet.

I left the office early, strangely excited about the evening ahead. By the time I arrived home, Sophie was, to my surprise, nearly ready.

She certainly looked it. I was often amazed that time hadn't dulled the thrill that I felt when I was with her. Her long dark hair was tied back with odd tendrils falling down to brush the striking features of her face. A tiny amount of eyeliner emphasised the seductive power of her pale blue eyes, wide and welcoming.

'Yes, here I am, all ready for you, darling.' She laughed, amused at my surprise that she was on time.

I opened the car door for her, not missing the chance to admire the shape of her lithe figure. She had dressed to impress. She was wearing tight black leggings cut off just below the knee and a crimson blouse tied back to expose the smooth brown skin of her stomach. Some fashionable high-heeled sandals added unnecessarily to her height and she climbed with ease into the Land Rover.

We had a lovely evening at the Horseshoes. The food was typical of British pub cuisine and arrived in a plastic basket but that didn't detract from the ambience of sitting out by the river and at least we were able to buy a bottle of half-decent wine. We chatted inconsequentially until well after closing time, thoroughly absorbed in one another's company until we were disturbed by distant shouts from the barman.

'Glasses, please,' echoed across the lawn. 'Time, ladies and gentlemen.'

I didn't want the evening to end. It had been lovely to be

out with Sophie, and reminiscent of the times we had spent together when we were courting. At least there wasn't the faint worry of wondering whether she'd want to come out again or the rigmarole of deciding how many days to leave it before telephoning her.

The following day I began my investigations into Trevor Castle. If he was making blue movies, Sir Charles wouldn't want him on the estate. I decided that my first point of call would be the Internet, a recent innovation in the estate office only agreed to by Sir Charles when I explained the cost was that of a local phone call. I tapped the words Trevor and Castle into the search engine. The reply came back that there were 1,026 page references. I began to surf through them. There was Trevor Castle, a Baptist minister in Alabama, Trevor Castle, a geography teacher in Alaska, Trevor Castle, an adolescent weirdo from South Yorkshire. In fact, there was all manner of Trevor Castles, but none of them seemed to be connected to the world of pornography. My only slight hope was Trevor Castle Films Ltd but the web page provided little information and what was there seemed perfectly innocent.

My initial investigations had revealed nothing concrete but I wasn't prepared to give up so easily. I decided that my next move should be to visit the video shop in town. I had often gone in there with Sophie to hire films for an evening. We would curl up in front of the television with a bottle of wine and spend the evening relaxing, usually in front of a romantic comedy if Sophie had her way. This time my mission was somewhat different.

Fortunately the shop was empty so I didn't feel self-conscious about being seen in the adult section. Having searched among the shelves for some time and seen nothing suspicious I decided I would have to go up to the counter.

A surly youth with matted hair and a ring through his eyebrow looked up.

'Yes, mate.'

'I am looking for a video by Trevor Castle Films. Do you have one?'

'Trevor Castle Films. Never heard of them. Are you sure you've got the right name?'

'Yes, I think so.'

'I s'pose I can look it up on the computer, if you like. Doubt it'll be there though. I know all the films in this shop.'

'Thank you.'

Using only one finger he slowly tapped in the letters.

'I'm wrong mate, we 'ave got some. I've got *Trevor's Bouncing Castles*, *Trevor's Bouncing Castles 2* and *Give It To Me Hardcastle*. I didn't realise it was adult films you were after. That's why I haven't heard of 'em.'

'I'll take all of them.'

You can't. I've only got *Trevor's Bouncing Castles 2* in stock. The others are on hire until next week.'

'I'll take that one then.'

He gave me a superior look, presumably imagining that I was a sad and lonely individual with nothing better to do with my evenings than watch dirty films while he, no doubt obliged to stand behind the counter until ten o'clock, was having the time of his life.

'That'll be £1.50 then, sir. Enjoy your evening,' he leered.

I hurried away, certain that the only enjoyment I would get would be if there was anything in the film to incriminate the new tenant of the Old Rectory.

When I arrived home I saw that Sophie had left a note on the kitchen table to say that she had gone to the tennis club and to join me there if I wanted to play. But much as I would have enjoyed a game I had important work to do.

I inserted *Trevor's Bouncing Castles 2* into the video recorder, pressed the play button and sat back on the sofa. To my annoyance I found that the tape was fuzzy, and although you could hear plenty of grunting and groaning you couldn't see the picture at all. I forwarded it all the way to the end of the tape but still there was nothing. As a final resort I rewound the tape but kept my index finger on the play button at the same time. This achieved a limited amount of success as now I could see the picture but all the action was in reverse. I was able to take in a particularly buxom girl with dyed-blonde hair getting out of bed and putting her clothes on at high speed and the same blonde jumping up and down on a trampoline in a garden while an equally naked and pneumatic brunette encouraged her from the side. Suddenly I realised I had made my breakthrough. Beyond the two girls I could see some wisteria stretching along the red bricks of the garden wall. I forwarded and rewound the film once again. This time I noticed the rhododendron bed at the foot of the wall. Each time I rewound the video I became more certain that filming had taken place in the garden of the Old Rectory.

'What on earth are you doing?'

I hadn't heard Sophie come in, so intent had I been on watching the video.

'Oh, hi,' I said, jumping up. 'I've been watching this video filmed at the Old Rectory. You remember the bloke I told you about – suspecting him of making blue movies? Well, I've got the answer.'

Chapter 18

The good weather held and the day of the Carnival dawned fine and dry with the promise of soaring temperatures. Sophie had come over for the day's festivities and we walked up to the square at midday where the carnival float procession was gathering. This year there seemed to be a larger turnout than usual – about twenty village organisations had entered, from the scout group to the pubs.

Masses of people milled around the square. Almost all the locals were there together with a good number of tourists. The Frampton Carnival had become well known in the area and each year brought a greater crowd than the last.

I watched the procession move off before I had to rush up to the playing field to meet Sir Charles. The theme of the carnival was music and the first float, carried on the back of Dennis Catchpole's brother-in-law's lorry, had a very lively West Indian band playing some steel drums. They were the organised entertainment for the day and, I suspect, more appropriate to Notting Hill than Frampton. The Kings Head had built a display depicting *The Rocky Horror Picture Show*, the theme music blasting out through some speakers, accompanied by a surprisingly well-choreographed dance routine. The Salvation Army had their brass band, the football, cricket and tennis clubs had all entered, their athletic members participating in somewhat more lively activities than the Women's Institute, who did what they did every year irrespective of the theme. They sat on chairs, singing. The Weavers' Guild, a jolly bunch of rosy-faced old ladies dressed in smocks, had a pen of sheep on their trailer, and were singing 'Baa Baa Black Sheep'. The Frampton Caged Bird Society had dressed up as parrots, with a recording of bird song just about audible from a cassette player dangling off a perch. The last float in the procession was an offering by the Antiques Centre, a shop that comprised of various traders under the one roof. Several highly embarrassed middle-aged men and women were prancing around a maypole balanced on the back of a lorry. Their gait was somewhat stilted, possibly because Miss Lamplight, who ran the centre, had taken part, and her eighty-year-old legs didn't achieve much speed as they circumnavigated the pole.

Riveted by the spectacle I had left only just enough time to get up to the playing field in front of them. Sir Charles was looking his best despite the well-worn tweed suit. As was his privilege he had parked his Morris Traveller in everybody's way next to the commentary caravan. Hole was standing next to it, having accompanied Sir Charles and his poodles to the event.

We waited for the floats to arrive and they then paraded in front of Sir Charles' judicious eye across the showring. He would spend all afternoon judging the events, which ranged from the best float to the tastiest apple pie to the under-fives egg-and-spoon race to the most obedient dog. There were competitions to suit all tastes and ages including, for the first time, the most amusingly shaped vegetable.

I introduced Sir Charles to Mr Flower, the organiser. We started with a tour of the floats and Sir Charles would offer some complimentary remark and occasionally mutter something less encouraging to me.

'Jolly good of you chaps to turn out,' he shouted at the steel band still strutting away on the lorry. 'Can't think what a bunch of Negroes banging some old oil drums have got to do with an English country fete,' he added under his breath.

He was captivated by the Rocky Horror show, the girls dressed as tarts and the men as transvestites. 'They're really men are they?' he said. 'Good heavens.'

Miss Lamplight had retired from the maypole dance, having nearly fallen off the lorry, and their dance routine had picked up speed. Meanwhile, some of the ladies from the Women's Institute had gone to sleep.

'Same as usual,' he whispered in my ear.

The battery on the Caged Bird cassette player had run out and the parrots stood mournfully quiet.

'What's this here?' barked Sir Charles. 'A pen of sheep!'

'Weavers' Guild,' I explained.

'Damn good idea,' he commented before moving on.

With great deliberation and much talk about the difficulty of judging he commended all the floats on their hard work before awarding the prize to the King's Head and its portrayal of the Rocky Horror Show.

'Great ingenuity,' he explained, 'and a bloody nerve to stand up there dressed as a queer,' he added to me.

'A most remarkable turnout, I must say,' he continued to the crowd, 'most remarkable indeed.'

I had no further duties as such and wandered around the ground to meet up with Sophie and the two of us meandered past the huge variety of side shows and exotic stalls. A loud woman of Rubenesque proportions stood by a coconut shy plying her wares. 'Fifty pence for three throws, dear,' she screamed. 'Take a coconut home with yer.' Another stall offered you the chance to toss a ping pong ball into a jam jar and win a goldfish, which could be relied upon to die within the week. There was an apple bobbing competition surrounded by a lot of excited children with wet hair, a guess the weight of the fruit cake competition, a raffle, a tombola and all the other traditional activities one would expect to find at an English fete.

Grandparents sat on straw bales by the showring seemingly captivated by the displays of falconry, football and sheepdog trials. Children tore around with excited squeals wanting to try everything whilst their parents struggled valiantly to keep smiling despite incessant pleas for candy floss.

The younger set of the village congregated in the beer tent amongst much jollity and laughter. I saw Trevor Castle holding court with a large group of people, predominantly blonde girls I noted. No doubt he was lining them up for his next film. I was tempted to go and confront him there and then. But it wouldn't have been appropriate to cause a scene at the Carnival, one of the most important dates in Frampton's social calendar. The matter could wait until our meeting next week.

I saw nearly all the villagers: Miss Hardcastle peering intently at an old plate on a second-hand stall; Mr and Mrs Taylor affecting not to notice their dog relieving himself against the beer tent; Dennis thrashing about with his shepherd's crook; Mr Thwaite, hopefully not intending to put a ferret down his trousers again; Mrs Ellis, having abandoned her neighbourhood watch; and even Fred Turner fully recovered from his fall and in the height of his bantam breeding season. Sir Charles was in his element. He loved these events, not because he was self important but because they represented the solid traditional English way of life that he knew and loved.

I was extremely surprised when I was tapped on the shoulder and turned around to find Sebastian standing there. He hadn't been expected, so far as I knew, and his reclusive character did not fit easily into such public adventures. Adding to my astonishment was his companion. A tall, striking looking girl in her early twenties I hadn't met her before but she certainly looked familiar.

'Hallo, Sebastian,' I said, pleased to see him. 'How are you?'

'Hallo,' he replied. 'I'm well, thank you. Down for the weekend as my father probably told you. Actually we weren't due until tomorrow but Serena wanted to get away from Cambridge so here we are. Meet Serena. Serena, this is James, my father's agent, and Sophie, his wife.'

We shook hands and exchanged pleasantries. Now that I had placed Serena I wondered quite how Sir Charles was going to take this. I had recognised her from the pages of *Hello!* and *OK*, magazines which Sophie sometimes brought home. I knew that she had something of a reputation as a party animal and had left a string of boyfriends in her wake. She seemed a most unlikely partner for Sebastian, for whom, as far as I knew, this was his first girlfriend.

'Um, well, I hope that you enjoy the fete,' I stuttered, taken aback by this turn of events. 'You'll find it very traditional. Do you also live in Cambridge?' I asked politely.

'No, not me. London's much more convenient,' she replied, in tones more often heard in Chelsea than rural Suffolk. I wondered what she would make of the Carnival, which was surely rather different from the A-list parties she was used to attending.

'Well, everybody's very friendly here,' I continued, 'so I'm sure you will enjoy the afternoon.'

'I'm sure we will, thank you, James,' said Sebastian, who seemed to be more confident in his manner than I remembered. 'By the way, I don't know if my father invited you to lunch tomorrow but I'd like you both to come if you can.'

This was a huge departure from the norm. Only once or twice had we eaten with the family, such as it was, but never at the behest of Sebastian. Hooked enquiringly at him.

'Do you think that is all right with your father, hadn't you better ask him first?'

'No. I would like you to be there. It will be fine with my father. I shall arrange it.'

Having only known him as a shadow of his father his newfound determination was disconcerting.

'Come,' he said, 'we'll go and meet him now,' and he strode off in the direction of the caravan where Sir Charles could be seen talking to a lady with blue hair and a poodle.

'Sebastian,' he cried in delight, 'I'm just talking to Mrs Witherspoon about her dog. Breeds poodles so we have something in common.'

'We do indeed, Sir Charles,' she beamed.

'Father, I'd like you to meet Serena,' Sebastian continued, guiding her forward into a melee of dogs.

'How do you do?' cried Sir Charles, who I suspected had been plied with copious amounts of whisky.

There was an embarrassed pause while Mrs Witherspoon, detecting her presence was not required, moved herself out of the group.

'Oh,' he said somewhat surprised. 'Er, are you one of his students?'

'No, Sir Charles,' Serena replied, smiling at Sebastian, 'we're good friends.'

'Oh, splendid,' boomed Sir Charles, having regained his composure quickly. 'Well now, um, Sarah . . .'

'Serena,' interrupted Sebastian.

'I'm sorry. Serena. Let me show you around. Um, how about the coconut shy. Let's go over there. Maybe win a coconut,' he added excitedly. 'Yes, come with me.'

Sir Charles, for all his oddities, could recognise a pretty girl when he saw one. Serena must have been nearly six feet tall and had the figure and facial structure of a supermodel. It wasn't lost on him. What was lost on him was who she was. Clearly Sir Charles and Sophie did not subscribe to the same magazines.

I held back with Sebastian. 'Is she all right alone with him?' I asked. 'I don't mean to be rude but you know that you're father takes a bit of getting used to.'

'Don't worry about her. Serena can hold her own with anybody. And I warned her what to expect.'

To my surprise, Sebastian was right. Within a short time Serena had Sir Charles proudly leading her around the fete as though he had organised the whole thing.

Chapter 19

The church was full the following morning, the congregation swelled by the number of visitors to the village.

Frampton's church was one of the famous 'wool churches' built in the late 1400s when East Anglia had been the wealthiest part of the country. The wealth was based on the production of wool and woollen cloth and the lord of the manor – Sir Charles' ancestor – and the wealthy burgesses of the town had funded the construction of a magnificent church. It was a thanksgiving to God for the victory of the Tudors at the Battle of Bosworth in 1485. The present church was a magnificent example of the Late Perpendicular period and stood on the highest point of the hill overlooking the village. Its 141 foot tower was visible from miles around.

Sir Charles and Sebastian, accompanied by Serena, occupied the lord of the manor's pew at the front. A little door blocked the entrance of lesser mortals to the pew. Sophie and I sat in the agent's pew on the other side of the aisle but were aware that Serena's presence was causing some lively interest.

The vicar was beside himself at having almost a full house. Now approaching retirement he normally presided over a few old faithfuls, having long since given up the struggle to attract a broader cross-section of the community. In

Frampton it was not always the case that time waits for no man as the gift of the priest's living was still in Sir Charles' hands. In effect this meant that the church was run as he liked.

Normally, Sophie and I were the youngest members of the congregation by about forty years and there didn't seem to be much hope of any younger people joining in. The Reverend Sidebottom's efforts to make the church appeal to Frampton's youth now extended only as far as a plastic cup of instant coffee and a plain digestive biscuit after the service. I was sure that if he offered alcopops and skateboarding down the main aisle attendances would soon treble but perhaps this was not compatible with his ministry.

On this occasion he had at least chosen some good rousing hymns, the sort that he knew Sir Charles enjoyed. Anything complicated or modern was a non-starter as the organist was a lady of limited musical ability. As it was she often struck the wrong note, reducing the singing to a whisper until she got back on track again. But today, with the church so full the enthusiastic singing from the crowd drowned out the organ and any mistakes were inaudible.

The Buckleys departed immediately after the service but we stayed for a few minutes, dutifully swapping pleasantries over cups of coffee. The Reverend Sidebottom shuffled over to me, his cassock somehow restricting his ability to walk properly.

'Absolutely lovely congregation this morning,' he enthused. 'So delightful to have all these young people here as well. Lovely to see you too, Mrs Aden.'

'Thank you,' Sophie replied. 'It is very full,' she agreed. 'It must make your job so much more exciting having the chance to address this many people.'

'Indeed it does, Mrs Aden, indeed it does. And how

charming to see Mr Sebastian with an escort for once. A lovely girl, lovely girl. Very tall.'

'Yes,' I said.

'And Mr Sebastian such a lovely man I always think. Such a shame he's not here more often but I gather he's very busy at the university.'

'So I understand, Mr Sidebottom. Very involved with research I believe.'

'Lovely man, lovely man,' he repeated again.

'Er, well, I hope you enjoyed the Carnival yesterday,' I offered, changing the subject.

'Oh, absolutely lovely,' he said. 'My sister was here and we had a lovely day. Such marvellous weather of course. My sister's from Frinton, you know, by the sea. A lovely place, lovely. But she likes to come inland occasionally.'

'And here's as good as anywhere I suppose,' I suggested.

'Oh, she thinks it's lovely. Says the same thing every time.'

Must be a family trait I thought as I decided it was time to get going. 'Well, I must get on now, Vicar. I'll see you next Sunday if not before.'

We drove up to the Hall for twelve-thirty. Hole answered the door and showed us through to the library where Sir Charles, Sebastian and Serena were having drinks. Hole poured dry sherry and withdrew.

After the usual pleasantries, Sir Charles launched straight into the point of the lunch with his normal brusqueness.

'Glad you're here, James and Sophie,' he said, 'Sebastian's got engaged to be married!'

I must have looked surprised, as indeed I was at this sudden and unlikely event.

'To Serena,' he added unnecessarily.

I collected my wits quickly. 'Congratulations to you

both,' I said, shaking hands with them. 'I have to admit it's a bit of a surprise, but no doubt a welcome one.'

'Oh, how wonderful,' said Sophie, grasping Serena's hand.

'Thank you,' said Sebastian, 'yes, it is a bit of a surprise, I think even to us!' He put his hand on Serena's arm, 'And especially for my father of course.'

I wondered how Sir Charles had taken it. He was desperate for Sebastian to get married, produce an heir and take an interest in the family's estates. On the other hand he had only met Serena the previous day and hardly knew anything about her. He must surely be worried that she might be a gold digger. He would certainly have been aware that Sebastian's innocence would make him easy prey. 'I've asked Hole to serve champagne with luncheon,' he barked, 'so that we can celebrate with a toast.'

'That is very kind of you, Sir Charles,' said Serena, astute enough to realise that her prospective father-in-law was finding the situation difficult.

'But first I want to show James some papers in my study, so if you'll excuse us for a few minutes.'

'Excuse me,' I said to the others, following Sir Charles who had shot out of the room. I walked quickly after him and caught him in the study pouring himself a Scotch.

'Help yourself,' he offered, absent-mindedly waving a hand in the direction of a drinks tray. 'There are papers of course,' he continued, 'but I would like to have a word with you in private.'

I waited for him to continue as he knocked back his drink in one swallow.

'I'm bound to say this has all come as a huge shock,' he said, choosing his words carefully. 'You're one of the few young people I know and you're about the same age as Sebastian. That is why I feel you're the best person I can talk to about it.'

'Thank you for your confidence, Sir Charles,' I replied. 'I'm sure it is a huge surprise.'

'My shock is twofold,' he continued, 'although I have had time to consider the matter since last night when they told me of their intentions. Firstly, Sebastian's getting married and that's a damn good thing. About bloody time. But I don't know the girl and I realise I shouldn't say this, but she's not from good stock.'

'Isn't she, Sir Charles?'

'Well, no, she isn't. As soon as I heard her surname, Cordle, I got the jitters.'

He poured himself another drink. I waited for him to continue but there was silence. Finally, he spoke again.

'Yes, Cordle. Been looking them up in Debrett's. There's no money there you know. Her father blew all, or most of it, on heroin before it finished him off. And her grandfather shot his own brains out. Couldn't handle the war apparently.'

'Well, I'm sure you have a point, Sir Charles, but they do seem very happy together. What's more it does seem to mean that at long last the future of your estate is secure.'

'That's true, I suppose,' said Sir Charles, demanding more reassurance.

'Well, I'm sure Sebastian would be certain that Serena is right for him before asking her to marry. He must be well aware of the importance of picking the right partner, not just for himself but for Frampton itself.'

There is all that but do you realise,' he blurted out, 'that she just spends her life going to parties? I've been picking Hole's brains. He reads one of those tabloids you know, and he tells me she's never done a day's work in her life.

Sebastian's a very serious young man. I can't see that they've got anything in common at all.'

'Well, trying to be positive, Sir Charles,' I responded, 'perhaps that doesn't matter. Maybe they can draw strength from their differences. Serena can support Sebastian socially and he can be an anchor for her. Besides, surely you should judge Serena on how you find her, not by what Hole has read in the papers or by her ancestors?'

'That's what we do with our livestock,' he grumbled. 'But perhaps you're right. Maybe we'll learn more about her at luncheon. Why do things have to be so bloody complicated? He could have chosen someone more, I don't know, one of my friend's daughters for instance.'

'You like her though, don't you?' I tried to diffuse his consternation. 'You seemed to enjoy her company yesterday.'

He strode over to the window overlooking the parkland sweeping down towards the lake. He stood there, as generations of his forebears must have done, motionless for several minutes, only the steady tick-tock of a longcase clock breaking the silence. At length he turned around.

'Yes,' he said forcefully, almost in surprise, 'I like her. Let's have luncheon.'

Sir Charles was a man of obsessive determination. Once he had a view on something he stuck to it with dogged conviction. He didn't care a jot what anyone else thought, you could see that from his opinions on politics, his car, the clothes he wore, and I sensed that once he had come to terms with Sebastian and Serena he would embrace the situation with his usual vigour.

Luncheon was a typically formal affair with Hole and a footman waiting at table. The five of us sat in a rather odd seating arrangement but one that I had been party to on previous occasions. Sir Charles sat at the head of the table, under one of the great Rembrandt portraits, and Sebastian sat about thirty feet away at the other end.

Sophie and I sat alongside each other, though ten foot part, with Serena opposite my wife. It could hardly have been described as intimate. The conversation eventually flowed, despite the need to shout in order to be heard.

'How did you meet each other?' I asked Serena, to break the ice.

'What was that?' barked Sir Charles. 'I couldn't hear.'

'I wondered how they'd met,' I shouted.

'Oh, yes, how they met,' he repeated.

'At a charity ball,' Serena replied, her vowels rounded to perfection. 'I help to organise them. Sebastian had been dragged along against his will by an old schoolfriend.'

She paused to look at Sir Charles, who beamed at her encouragingly.

'Glad I went now, of course,' Sebastian continued. 'Not many men can say they met their wife while saving the rainforest. Even if I was in London at the time.'

'I'm not your wife yet.' Serena smiled coquettishly.

'Soon though,' Sebastian beamed back.

'I had no idea you organised balls,' boomed Sir Charles.

'Oh, I thought Sebastian would have told you.'

'Do you enjoy it?' Sophie asked, joining in the conversation.

'I find it very rewarding. It took me a long time to find my place. Daddy dying so young meant that I lost my moorings for a while. But then I realised that the point of the trust fund wasn't to spend it as quickly as possible. I knew then that I wanted to help others so a couple of girlfriends and myself got together to organise these charity balls. We have got good contacts in the celebrity magazines so we get plenty of publicity as well.'

This was much more promising, I thought to myself. The more she spoke the more she seemed to be the perfect partner for Sebastian. Beautiful, outgoing, amusing, but with a seriousness about her, she was just what Frampton needed.

The conversation moved away from an inquisition and on to more general topics. Sir Charles' conversation was really meant to encourage Sebastian to take more of an interest in the estate.

'Found a new hatchery to send us poults,' he bellowed down the table, referring to a supply of pheasant chicks for the shoot.

'Barley's coming orf a bit light,' he said when we'd exhausted the pheasant conversation. 'It's going to be a difficult harvest this year, mark my words.'

I think he was telling Serena that 'his favourite hunter had thrown a splint' when Sebastian suggested that we withdraw to the library for coffee.

Sir Charles wanted to show Serena some of the house and with much aplomb steered her and Sophie in the direction of the Long Gallery. Sebastian and I went through to the library where Hole had laid out coffee.

'What did father say before lunch?' he asked me.

'Not a lot really. He has been surprised by the turn of events. More so than he's probably let on.'

'I know. And I should maybe have given him more warning. But I didn't want to give him the chance to pre-judge Serena before he met her. I thought it would be better in the long run just to spring her on him and see how he reacted. She's been brilliant though I did warn her it would be difficult.'

'Well, he seems pleased to me. As am I, of course.'

'It's been the most extraordinary thing all this,' Sebastian went on. 'I had accepted that I would never get married and was happy just being involved with my work at Cambridge. The women I met never interested me, especially the ones thrown at me by their mothers. Then about a year ago I met Serena and for no reason I fell for her. I still don't know why but it doesn't matter. I couldn't be happier.'

I wondered how their lives would change.

'Do you intend to live here or stay on at Cambridge?' I asked him.

'I think we'll come back here,' he said. 'I won't give up my work so I expect we'll keep my house in Cambridge and depending on father, stay here for part of the time.'

'That's all a bit far in the future I suppose,' I said, 'but one thing you'll have to do soon is change your car. You can't expect Serena to go around in that three-wheeler thing of yours.'

He laughed. 'No, I think that has had its day.'

'How did you get here?'

'Oh, in a taxi. But don't mention that to my father. He'll think I'm being led into a life of extravagance already. I don't think he's ever been in a taxi in his life!'

Sir Charles and the girls returned from their tour and after coffee Sophie and I left them to their family gathering. I could see from the glint in his eye that all his qualms had been put to rest. Sebastian was getting married and the future of Frampton was now assured.

By mid-morning the following day things appeared a great deal less assured. Frampton was full of tourists for the Bank Holiday and Brigadier Hand's careful arrangements for the gymkhana, had, to excuse the pun, got out of hand.

Whilst matters on the field itself were running impeccably, the congested road into the village had been blocked by a

Land Rover and horsebox. Having overshot the turning, a decidedly flustered young mother was trying to reverse the vehicle but had now managed to wedge it in a narrow gap between two parked cars. I recognised that one of the cars belonged to the landlord of the Anne of Cleves, the other must have been a visitor's – guessing by the sticker in the rear window announcing, CITY SLICKERS DO IT IN THEIR KNICKERS. I wasn't going to guess what but suspected they might when they saw how close the horsebox was to their gleaming Mercedes.

I went over to the agitated mother. Her distress was not helped by an overexcited child in the back seat screaming nor the alarmed pony in the trailer lunging about in fright. Hearing the noise and pandemonium in the street, someone had astutely found the pub landlord who arrived to move his car. After helping her negotiate the way out I made my way down to the gymkhana field in the park.

Many families had already arrived and were sitting around on picnic rugs whilst their young children were trotting their ponies briskly up and down the field.

The Brigadier had established a command post in a lurid yellow caravan, stationed beside the ring. If the colour of the caravan wouldn't make the ponies shy then his experiments with the tannoy system would. Some ear-piercing screeches ensued before he finally managed to gain control.

Once I was sure that I could approach the caravan without being deafened, I walked over and tried to open the door. It wouldn't budge so I knocked.

'Come in,' boomed the Brigadier across the showground.

'I can't', I replied loudly, in deference to his poor hearing, 'I think it's locked.'

'No, it's not locked,' he informed everyone. 'I think the bally thing's a bit warped. Wait a sec . . .'

Without warning the Brigadier gave it an almighty kick from inside, slamming the door in my face.

'That's the job,' he shouted, now attracting considerable interest from followers of the Pony Club. 'Ah, Aden, it's you, old chap – heavens man, you're covered in blood. What's happened to you?'

'You just kicked the door in my face,' I muttered, trying to stem the blood. 'I think I've got a nosebleed.'

'Who's kicked you in the face?' he cried in alarm. 'A pony?'

'No, never mind, Brigadier. It's simply a mistake. I didn't expect the door to open so suddenly.'

'I'll get the St John Ambulance people over,' he suggested. 'That's what they're here for.'

In fact, alerted by the tannoy, they were already on their way. So was half the crowd.

'Brigadier, could you take the microphone off your lapel? We're live on air.'

'I can see blood in your hair,' he agreed. 'Some of these ponies are little blighters, the sods.'

My nosebleed was easing and with the impending arrival of ambulancemen I was more concerned that the broadcast was finished.

'Could you turn off the microphone?' I yelled, pointing at his lapel.

He looked blankly at me for a few seconds before the penny finally dropped.

'Great Scott,' he exclaimed. 'Is this thing on?'

He launched himself back into the caravan and several ear-splitting screeches later reappeared looking slightly chastened.

'You know, Aden,' he barked, 'I used to be much more reliable with those hand-held trumpet things. Knew where you were with them.'

By now the ambulancemen had arrived and kindly cleaned the worst of the blood from my face. No lasting damage had been done although I suspected I'd have a black eye in the morning.

'You'd better come in and have a tot of whisky, my dear fellow,' the Brigadier suggested. 'Looks like you need it.'

I accepted gratefully and climbed into the yellow box behind him.

I sat down beside a large box of multicoloured rosettes while he poured a generous tumbler of malt. The vulgarity of his base camp clearly didn't mean he was going to let his personal standards slip.

I had no official part to play in the afternoon's proceedings and my visit was purely to show some support. So after a while recuperating with the Brigadier's whisky, I left for a stroll around the gymkhana.

I daresay the drink was partly to blame but my enthusiasm for watching gawky little girls charging about on fat little ponies waned within the hour. Even the spectacle of the egg and spoon race held scant attraction and I soon departed for Cordwainers with the echoes of the Brigadier booming across the park.

Chapter 20

I happened to be in the post office the next morning and the place was full of old ladies cackling with gossip about Sebastian and Serena. Gradually a hush fell as one by one they noticed me.

Mrs Makepeace, the postmistress, couldn't have been more inappropriately named. For the cost of a second-class postage stamp one could glean as much local information as if one spent all day wandering the streets spying on the inhabitants. Nor was she hesitant in airing her views.

'I was just saying to Mrs Derby that Mr Sebastian's got himself engaged,' she said to me while Mrs Darby fumbled in her bag for nineteen pence.

'Yes, marvellous news isn't it, Mrs Makepeace,' I replied, bending down to retrieve Mrs Darby's walking stick, which had fallen on the floor. 'She's a lovely girl, should be a great asset around here.'

'Saw her in church,' continued Mrs Makepeace. 'An unusual choice I thought.'

'Presumably you're saying that because of her reputation?' I retorted sharply.

The postmistress looked at me. 'Yes,' she said. 'She's always in the papers. Doesn't seem the type for Mr Sebastian at all.'

'Mrs Makepeace. I have met Sebastian's fiancée, Serena. She is a delightful person, highly intelligent and interesting.

I have no doubt that she will be a huge asset to this community when eventually they settle here.'

'Me chimney pot's come orf,' interrupted Mrs Darby.

'What?'

'Fell orf and smashed to bits in me yard.'

'Have you rung the estate office about it?' I asked her.

'I'm telling you now.'

'Okay, I'll put it on the builder's list.'

'Me fire's smoking while you're at it.'

'I expect that's because the pot has broken, Mrs Darby.'

I turned back to Mrs Makepeace. 'There's no doubt, however, that she'll have quite a job settling in to such a grand estate as this. A lot of prejudices to overcome. Still, like it or not, one day she'll be the next Lady Buckley so people will do best to remember that.'

'You're right,' Mrs Darby agreed. 'They can ne'er do without the pot.'

Trevor Castle was waiting for me in the office, slightly early for our appointment. Gail, as to be expected, was fiddling around in the hall. She had obviously heard about the meeting as she had dressed for the occasion. For a farm secretary it was an unusual choice of attire and certainly one that left nothing to the imagination. Long black boots, a white skirt about the size of a paper table napkin, and a tight-fitting black top that appeared to me as though it might burst open at any time. Her make-up was artistically challenged and I couldn't help thinking that she resembled a rather fat panda.

They were startled to see me, not having heard my entrance.

'Morning, Gail, Mr Castle,' I interrupted. 'Everything all right? 'They stepped back from one another.

'Yes, fine thanks, James,' replied Gail, reddening.

'Come in, Mr Castle.' I led him into my office and drew out a chair. 'Please sit down.'

'Thank you,' he said as he briefly surveyed the room. For an office it was very lavishly decorated. Good oil paintings hung from the walls, a selection of fine eighteenth-century furniture graced the room and extravagant floor-length silk damask curtains framed the windows.

'Coffee?' I asked.

'Er, yes, thank you.'

I was determined to be civilised. It would make victory all the sweeter.

'You've got yourself quite a pad here,' he commented, standing up to take a closer look at some of the paintings. He singled out a study of a racehorse by Raoul Millais and much to my consternation ran a finger over its surface.

'Original, is it?' he asked in a manner that I associated with people in the motor trade.

'Yes, it's a stunning piece of work,' I said, 'my favourite actually.'

'Now that's what I call a stunning piece of work,' he quipped, pointing out of the window. 'That's class Al totty.'

Isobel was crossing the square.

'Wouldn't mind showing her round the Old Rectory.'

'I'm sure you wouldn't,' I said, concealing my disgust that he might want to entice the girl into one of his sordid films. 'I gather you have quite a crowd of women up there already.'

He laughed dismissively. 'Yeah, well, they just come and go, you know how it is. I like a bit of variety, change 'em every few weeks. Mind you that one's probably worth keeping a bit longer. Just look at her body.'

He sat down again as Anne brought in the coffee.

'Yeah, well, down to business. I think Gail mentioned

it to you. I want to rent that little field beside my house, to give me a bit more privacy. I'd give you a good price for it. A lot more than anyone else would pay.'

'I'm sorry, it's not available. The estate prefers to keep the field open to the public as a recreation ground. I believe this was explained to you when you first signed the contract on the Old Rectory. Anyway, to put it bluntly, Sir Charles doesn't need the money.'

'Yeah, but everything has its price, doesn't it?'

'It might in your business but it doesn't here,' I told him.

'What if I offered three times its value, you'd be a fool not to let me have it then,' he argued.

'I wouldn't be a fool,' I said slowly, 'there are long-term implications that we consider in all aspects of estate policy, and have considered here. I'm afraid that you will have to accept that the field is not available. If the situation ever changes then I will let you know.'

I was enjoying the conversation, reeling him in. For now I was on the defensive, fending off his rapier thrusts, but I knew that he would have no answer to my lunge when the time came for me to attack.

'I'm sorry,' I said, not sorry at all, 'but I really can't help you.'

'Can't or won't?'

I stared at him. 'What do you mean by that?'

'Well, we'll see,' he said, standing up.

'One thing before you go, Mr Castle.'

'What is it?'

'You are familiar with the terms of your agreement, aren't you?'

'I guess.'

'All the terms,' I queried.

'What are you getting at?'

'Can I draw your attention to clause five, point ten? The one that reads, "The tenant will not use the premises for any illegal or immoral or improper purpose."'

'What of it?'

'I think that the use of Sir Charles Buckley's land to make pornographic films constitutes improper purpose.'

'What are you suggesting? That I make dirty films?' He laughed.

'That's precisely what I'm suggesting, Mr Castle.'

'I work in the Internet business. I'm a respectable businessman,' he blustered.

I took out the copy of *Trevor's Bouncing Castles 2* and threw it across the desk.

'I believe you used the garden of the Old Rectory making this film.'

Suddenly Trevor Castle seemed much smaller of stature, the confidence with which he had entered village life drained from his face.

'Mr Castle, it's not going to take a court of law to determine an irremedial breach of your tenancy. However, I can be reasonable. If you vacate the Old Rectory within the next week the estate will take no further action against you. Now, I suggest you go home and start packing.'

'But . . .'

'Good day, Mr Castle.'

I rang Gail's extension.

'Gail, any chance you could come down for a minute, please?' I asked.

'Yeah, straightaway,' she squealed and appeared thirty seconds later. She looked forlornly around my office and the enthusiasm drained visibly from her.

'He's gone, has he? Trevor?'

'Yes, he's just left. I'm afraid we didn't have a very good

meeting,' I explained. 'Sit down for a moment.'

There was an unusual creaking sound as the panda outfit's tensile strengths were put under enormous pressure. I thought for a horrible moment that her bosom was going to break free and her skimpy top propel itself across the leather top of my mahogany desk.

'Yes, I'm afraid I've had to ask him to leave the Old Rectory and indeed Frampton altogether.'

'You're getting a bit ahead of yourself aren't you? However much you don't like him, you don't have the power to do that.'

'Gail, it's nothing to do with that. He's been making pornographic films up there. It's against the terms of his tenancy.'

'No! How did you find out?'

'Usual way. Faint rumour in the post office, a comment in the greengrocer's, scandalous details in the butcher's, you know the sort of thing.'

'My God, is it all over town?' she exclaimed.

'Probably, I shouldn't worry. If we took any notice of all the things said around here we'd never go out of the house.'

Suddenly Gail burst into tears. I went to put my arm round her but she pushed me away.

'I shouldn't cry about it. You've had a lucky escape. Just think how unhappy he would have made you.'

I knew that I would never work for Relate but I was surprised at the ferocity of the bauling my soothing words engendered. Gail tried to speak but her sobs kept getting in the way. Finally she managed a decipherable mutter.

'James,' she said, 'you've got to help me.'

'Of course, anything I can do. But don't get too upset, I'm sure the right man will turn up for you.'

'You don't understand.'

'Yes, yes, I do. It's very hard when you think you've met the one and then they turn out to be someone else.'

'You don't understand. I've been seeing Trevor for the past week.'

'Oh . . . I see. Well, just be grateful it wasn't longer. Think how much harder it would be if you had been seeing him for months, years even.'

It made perfect sense to me but my words seemed to induce an even more desperate bout of wailing. Finally she blurted out,

'You don't understand. I let him film me. You've got to help.'

I was stunned. I knew that Gail was Frampton's sexual-liberation champion but to let a man she barely knew film her doing goodness knows what was taking things too far. There was only one thing for me to do. I had to get the pornographic tape back from Castle before it was too late. I called Anne in and asked her to look after Gail while I shot off to the Old Rectory.

'What do you want?' he asked aggressively as I stood at the door.

'This is a delicate matter. I understand you have a video cassette of Gail in, shall we say, a compromising position.'

'Sure I do.'

'Can I have it?'

There was an ominous silence as he weighed up the pros and cons of handing it over.

'The tape please, Mr Castle.'

He retreated into the hallway before returning with a small brown parcel.

'Enjoy it, won't you.'

'See you around, Mr Castle,' I replied, thankful that I would not.

When I returned to the office, Gail was still in floods of tears and there was no sign of her caterwauling abating. I gave her the tape.

'Thank you, James, thank you so much,' she sobbed. No one must ever know about this,' she added quietly, dabbing at her running mascara.

Tempted though I was to offer this now very sad looking panda a bamboo stick, I realised that Gail would not appreciate the joke and would probably prefer a little gallantry.

'Of course,' I replied sincerely.

Chapter 21

The weekend seemed a long way off and if Sebastian hadn't telephoned with some startling news the week would have dragged endlessly.

'I'm ringing from Cambridge,' he said with as much incredulity as if he'd found a telephone box in the Amazon jungle. He had clearly inherited his father's attitude towards modern conveniences.

'Are you?' I replied.

'Yes,' he said, 'from Cambridge. From the university.'

'Oh.'

'So I shall not speak for long.'

'Right. What can I do?'

'Serena and I have set a date for our wedding.' He told me when it was.

'But that's only six weeks away,' I said in surprise.

'I know,' he continued, 'but there are er, special reasons.'

'Oh, I see,' I said, the penny dropping. 'You mean that Serena's er . . .'

'Yes. We knew at the weekend of course, but thought it best to break all this bit by bit as it were.'

'Well, that's excellent, presumably you have told your father.'

'Yes. Actually we told him on Sunday before we left.'

'How did he take it?' I asked, feeling rather sorry for Sir Charles. It must have been one of the most alarming weekends of his life. His world had turned upside down within a matter of two days.

'He was delighted, much to my surprise. Quite honestly he has been so worried about heirs and all that sort of thing, he'd be happy with a monkey so long as it was related.'

'I suppose so,' I commented, not entirely sure that was correct. 'What do you need me to do?'

'I'm arranging a trustees' meeting on Tuesday,' he explained, 'with my father and the others. Could you come along at say eleven-thirty up at the Hall?'

'Of course,' I agreed.

'Good. I'll see you then.'

I had an appointment with Sir Charles later that morning and I thought that it might be useful to go over the subjects that were bound to come up at the trustees' meeting. I had no doubt that I would be asked to help with finding a house for Sebastian on the estate. The Old Rectory had already been snapped up so that was unavailable. In any case, perhaps Sir Charles had the Hall in mind.

I arrived in the middle of a commotion. A pigeon had got into the study, flown around the room in a panic knocking things over and left an extraordinary amount of bird mess on Sir Charles' desk. One of the poodles had caught the bird, scattering feathers everywhere. The excited poodle had then peed against the side of the sofa. Hole was fussing about the carnage whilst the baronet was peering intently at what appeared to be some bird droppings on the mantelpiece.

'Oh, dear, not such a good morning!' I said striding into the room. Both men looked up from what they were doing and stared mournfully at me.

'Bloody pigeon mess everywhere,' commented Sir Charles, 'let's go in the library.'

Hole's dispassionate expression never faltered. He was

kneeling on the floor, immaculately attired in his liveried tailcoat, picking up feathers.

'Could you get some coffee sent down when you've a moment,' asked Sir Charles.

'Very good, Sir Charles,' he responded and eased himself carefully off the floor.

The meeting with Sir Charles was not very constructive. He seemed to have forgotten all about Sebastian and was more interested in discussing the goings-on in the study.

'To put it bluntly, James,' he said, 'how on earth can so much shit come out of a bird that size?'

I was a bit taken aback at the question although admittedly the bird had made quite a mess.

'I don't know,' I responded lamely. 'Just as well it wasn't a, er, I don't know, a buzzard or something.'

'Heavens!' he exclaimed. 'We don't want a buzzard in there.' He paused. 'I remember a long time ago, when my wife was alive, a robin flew into her bedroom one morning. That caused a hell of a mess for its size. There must be something disproportionate between the size of a bird and its volume of excrement.'

I waited for a minute unsure of how to go on. I had hoped to get some idea of Sir Charles' plans regarding a house for Sebastian but he seemed to be preoccupied with bird droppings.

'Er . . . well, Sir Charles. Perhaps moving on, I thought we should have a word about next Tuesday's meeting with the trustees. I gather a wedding date has been set already and I wanted to know if there's anything you particularly wanted me to do.'

'Oh, yes, of course,' he said. 'It's all moving so fast with Sebastian. I'm pleased of course, no doubt about that. Trying to come to terms with it all. This time last week you know, none of us had an inkling. And now, wedding, wife, even child on its way. Extraordinary. I think the wedding they'll sort out themselves, have a little reception here I expect. But we do need to find them a house. Have you any thoughts on that?'

'I wondered whether you'd consider modernising the west wing for them. You don't really need it yourself do you?'

Sir Charles looked aghast.

'Oh, I don't think that's a good idea at all,' he spluttered in anguish. 'There wouldn't be room for all of us what with a new family on its way and all that. No. No. Not a good idea at all.'

'I just thought it was a sensible use of that part of the house, Sir Charles. I mean there's over sixty bedrooms and you only use one.'

'No. I think we'd feel we were living on top of one another. The noise and all that sort of thing.'

I felt like pointing out that the west wing was in fact a quarter of a mile away from the apartments Sir Charles used but clearly the thought of sharing was a non-starter.

'We need to find a good house on the estate. Pity there's no dower house as such. What about Bull Place Farmhouse? Who's in there now?'

'That's a possibility. People called Smith live there but we can move them elsewhere. It needs complete modernising though,' I explained.

'Well, see what Sebastian thinks.'

Hole arrived with the coffee, slightly out of breath.

'Coffee, Sir Charles,' he said.

'Thank you, Hole. How's my study.'

'We're just finishing now, I'm pleased to say. Mrs Jubb is in there with her cleaning utensils.'

'Excellent,' boomed Sir Charles. 'Bloody pigeon. Now

where were we, James? Ah, yes, a house. We'll talk to Sebastian next week.'

He rambled on about minor estate matters – the size of the young pheasants, rabbits getting into the kitchen garden and then abruptly decided the meeting was at an end.

I went off in search of Hole and found him in the butler's pantry cleaning some silver with great deliberation.

'Better than clearing up bird's muck!' I joked but his deadpan expression didn't falter.

'There are a wide variety of tasks involved in running a house of this size,' he said, 'and this is one of the more mundane.'

I drove back down to the office and settled down to a pile of paperwork. Everything we did on the estate seemed to involve copious amounts of paper, forms, letters, reports, minutes always seemed to be required. I often wondered why people couldn't just do things. Physically get on and do them instead of pontificating about some idea for weeks beforehand.

I had in front of me a typically useless missive from a nontenant who lived next door to one of the estate cottages let to a young couple who worked in the village. This was the third such letter from Mr and Mrs F Walsh. It had one of those ghastly address stickers at the top which always gave a clue to the sender's social standing. Usually somewhere between a lorry driver and a junior administrative assistant in the local council. It also usually indicated people who spent too much of their leisure time writing letters of complaint to everyone from the local newspaper to the environmental health officer. The letter stated that 'the female member of the household currently residing in 24 Back Street (property belonging to the Frampton Hall Estate) makes clearly audible sounds at night, which we believe to be of a sexual nature. This is causing both my husband and myself some distress.'

I sat with the letter in my hand for a while reflecting on its contents. It was, I have to admit, somewhat more interesting than the Ministry of Agriculture forms, Health and Safety Bulletins on crop-spraying or even *Chartered Surveyor Monthly*. It was also outside my usual range of duties and bar writing back suggesting that they ask their neighbour to close the window, I didn't see what else I could do.

Chapter 22

With all the rushing around of our busy lives it was easy to miss out on the exciting, romantic things that Sophie and I used to do before we got married. I hadn't forgotten about my plans for a picnic and one Saturday we put everything else out of our minds and as a sort of surprise I prepared it for her. We were lucky with the weather as it was warm for a September day and the clear blue sky and sunshine enhanced the colours of the beginning of autumn. Still green, the leaves on the trees were beginning to take on a yellow hue, the corn fields were golden stubble or patches of plough, and the whole landscape was imbibed with a sense of calm after the energies of a season's growth. Quietly, without noticeable effort, nature was slipping towards its period of rest.

I had gone to some trouble over our picnic. I wanted to show that Sophie mattered, that she was worth an effort and that we would avoid the contempt of familiarity just because we were married. I went shopping the day before and bought champagne, cream cheese wrapped in smoked salmon, a game terrine with cranberry sauce and a fresh chocolate roulade. It was a rich but seductive meal. That was only part of it. The chosen place was just as important.

There had always seemed to me to be a great art in wooing a girl, a species with such a complicated nature that it was impossible to fathom. To catch one, a good one, was as challenging as landing a fine salmon. One can cast a rod for hours, days even, over the tumbling waters of a Scottish river, trying different flies and yet knowing all the time that the fish don't feed during their passage up stream. Suddenly a mighty fish, a beautiful, silvery, speckled prize of the river, will be on the hook and away with it in his mouth. They run, they turn, hide under rocks, jump and race off again playing games with you. The skill is playing with them until eventually they succumb and glide calmly into a landing net. Just like girls. When to strike is critical with both. Too quickly and they're frightened off, too slowly and they're bored, lured away by another distraction. Just because we were married didn't make it less challenging.

I had chosen the place carefully, a secluded sunlit glade with wide open views to the south across the rolling landscape of Suffolk which I had ridden through a few weeks previously. The patchwork quilt of browns, golds and greens had been captured years before by Constable and preserved for immortality on his canvases. Now we could enjoy them for real and savour the warmth and smell of the landscape.

I had spread a rug over the thick carpet of springy grass, a natural mattress lfor us to sit on. We ate, talked and drank the champagne leisurely, enjoying each other's company in the intimacy of our hidden clearing in the wood.

After lunch we cleared the remnants away and lay back side by side, sipping the crisp dry wine and slowly mellowing because of its intoxicating effect. Suddenly we were in each other's arms, embracing fervently with an intensity born out of latent desire. The sexuality of Sophie's body, her skilful kissing and caressing were unsurpassable. We moved into an oblivion of our own, leaving the world behind. All afternoon we lay in the sunshine luxuriating in the warmth of its rays and our physical closeness.

When we gathered our things and made our way back to the Land Rover the passion immediately felt unreal. It was as though we had dreamt it and we didn't say much though the silence was tender and comforting. We returned to Cordwainers, neither one of us wanting to break the trance. Although it wasn't particularly cold I lit a fire and we cuddled together on the sofa relishing the warmth.

Built in the fourteenth century the house was heavily timbered with exposed oak beams lying at inconceivable angles in the wall and ceilings. The original timber frame of the house was obvious although over the centuries it had moved a little, producing oddities like the crooked window facing the driveway. Like many of the medieval buildings in the area it possessed immense charm and character.

I had found a suitable bottle of Château D'Issan, a full substantial claret from Saint Emillion, and we sat in front of the massive inglenook fireplace sipping the wine. The aroma of it was so intense that it brought back memories of time spent in France.

'Thees es very good, thees wine,' joked Sophie, her head on my shoulder. 'Even my father would approve and 'e es very particuleur with 'is wine.'

I tasted it again, relishing the flavour and could almost see the vineyards laid out in front of a château.

'It is good, isn't it? It makes me long for a trip to France. To sample its exquisite food and wine.'

'Well, we ought to go. One day we'll drive over there and explore the real France.'

We were now entwined on the sofa enjoying the claret. I kissed her lightly on the nape of her neck when suddenly there was a banging on the back door.

'Mr Aden, you in there? Me toilet's blocked,' screeched the voice of Mrs Painter.

I looked at Sophie.

'I'm sorry to bother you, Mr Aden, but it's blocked solid it is. Can ye 'ear me?'

I let go of Sophie and with an exasperated shrug of my shoulders went to the door.

'Hallo, Mrs Painter,' I said. 'Actually it's a little inconvenient for me to help just now. I'll give you the plumber's number,' I said, scribbling it down on a notepad that I kept by the back door. 'And I should ring straight away or he'll probably go out for the evening.'

She took the piece of paper and turning her ample frame carefully on the steps, rather like an ocean liner preparing to leave port, waddled off down the path.

Sophie Was giggling. 'That was bad timing, eh?' she laughed.

I smiled. 'At least you saw the funny side. Still, now We've been interrupted we may as well make some supper. Test your amazing French cooking skills,' I joked.

'We'll 'ave to see what you 'ave in 'ere,' she replied, starting to open cupboard doors. 'Ah, the refrigerateur!'

Sophie busied herself throwing pieces of this and bits of that on to the sideboard with Gallic abandon and accompanying comments.

'Where es the garlic?' she demanded. 'We es in a problem with no garlic!'

'Here,' I said.

'Voilà! You chop it. Very fine please.'

She crashed pans about, chopped, sliced, stirred, fried and within ten minutes the kitchen was filled with the delicious aromas of Provençal cooking.

We ended up with a fantastic melee of tomato, onions, garlic and olives fired with thin strips of lamb, all highly seasoned with herbs. She sautéed potatoes until they were crisp and salty, produced a salad of lettuce and chicory with a sublime dressing after pounding some herbs and more garlic in a pestle and mortar, added olive oil, lemon juice and whatever else she seemed to think appropriate, ending up with a concoction that made the lettuce almost a delicacy.

With that feeling only achievable by a cocktail of delicious food, good wine, a blazing log fire and devotion, we talked and laughed late into the evening. It seemed a natural progression to drift upstairs and lie together in our four-poster bed nestling under the eaves of the old house. Candlelight flickered softly, the dim yellow glow illuminating the uneven timbers against the whitewashed walls. Eventually, in the cocoon of our own little world, we slept.

Chapter 23

'There's something here for you from Sir Charles,' announced Anne as I arrived at the office. 'Looks like an invitation.'

'Oh,' I said, taking it from her. 'I wonder what it is? It's not like him to go sending out invitations.'

I opened the envelope, embossed on the back with his coat of arms. 'You're right,' I commented, 'it is an invitation. A reception to celebrate the forthcoming marriage of Sebastian and Serena, it says.'

'Wow!' exclaimed Anne. 'You are honoured. I wonder who else will be going.'

'Have to wait and see. Black tie, so it's formal.'

Sir Charles wouldn't have considered black tie as particularly formal. While he went about during the daytime in the most ancient of suits he dressed for dinner every evening whether entertaining or more commonly, eating on his own. I doubted that there were many gentlemen left nowadays who expected, as a matter of course, their dinner to be served by a butler and footman at a table that seated thirty people. The idea of dining in front of the television with a tray on his lap appalled him.

In due course, Sophie and I arrived at the Hall at the appointed hour. We were met by Hole at the south door and shown into the Wedgwood Room. With Wedgwood-blue walls, a ceiling fussily decorated with ornate white plasterwork and a marble floor it was easy to understand why the room was rarely used. It made you feel as though you were standing in an enormous fruit bowl. It was not the sort of room likely to make guests feel relaxed. Indeed, the assembled crowd were standing awkwardly as if attending a lecture in a museum.

As I glanced around it became clear why Sophie and I had been invited. There seemed to be hordes of Serena's friends and very few of Sebastian's. We were there to even up the numbers. Sir Charles was accompanied by a cousin of his late wife's, the dowager Duchess of Morieux. An imposing lady of impeccable breeding, I had met her a couple of times before as she was occasionally called upon to escort Sir Charles. I found her difficult to talk to as she was, I think, uncomfortable socialising with anyone ranking lower than a baronet. She was smoking a long thin cigar clasped in a pearl holder and had a pile of diamonds arranged in her hair. Her granddaughter, Lady Emma, a ravishing beauty but an awful snob, stood next to her. She was Sebastian's closest cousin and would, if Sebastian died childless, be the main beneficiary of the Buckley fortune. Its loss to her, however, would have been nothing more than a little disappointing as her father's fortune kept her in the lifestyle to which she had become accustomed. A confident young woman with a tendency to dismiss those who held no interest for her, she had the backside of a woman who spends too much time in the saddle.

Sir Charles came over and introduced me to an ungainly and nervous young man called Mr Nigel Sicklesmere, who was accompanying Lady Emma. Ill at ease in the assembled group, he was perspiring furiously, something I first noticed when we shook hands. Mr Sicklesmere thrust his clammy hand forward and then pumped my arm up and down as though he was inflating a bicycle tyre. The vigour of these actions caused him to spill his champagne on the floor and in his agitation the poor man stepped hurriedly back, knocking into Hole. A tray of hors d'oeuvres crashed on to the marble tiles with an almighty bang.

There was a moment's silence before Hole said, 'I am so sorry, sir. Please, let me fetch you a napkin.'

Mr Sicklesmere's face went as red as a beetroot and his embarrassment was not helped by Lady Emma unhelpfully whispering loudly, 'Nigel, you clumsy oaf.'

The duchess turned away to talk to Sebastian, oblivious to a prawn vol au vent stuck to the heel of her shoe.

Sir Charles, the ever-courteous host, ignored the drama and continued, 'James, I'm sure that you and Mr Sicklesmere will have much in common.'

As it turned out we didn't have anything in common, but I was intrigued to find out how he had become involved with Lady Emma.

'We met thwough a fwiend of mine who's going out with Emma's flatmate,' he explained.

'Oh, I see,' I said. 'And what do you do for a living?'

'I'm a libwawian,' he replied, 'in the Bwitish Libwawy. Histowical cataloguing mainly.'

'I expect you'd find the library here interesting then,' I suggested.

'I would, I'm sure. Emma's mentioned it to me. You pwobably know she wuns a business dealing in antiquawian books.'

'Actually, I'd forgotten. It explains why you two are together, doesn't it?'

'James,' interrupted Sir Charles, 'Yyou haven't met Colonel and Mrs Johnson and their daughter Belinda.'

I had heard of the Johnsons. They farmed a sizeable

spread on the outskirts of Bury St Edmunds and had established a renowned shoot to which Sir Charles was a frequent
guest. A chunk of their land had been sold off for housing
development and the resulting millions had enabled them to
increase the area of their farm considerably. Belinda Johnson
was going to need those millions, I thought uncharitably,
to attract a husband. She was as close as I'd ever seen to
a living Neanderthal man, complete with moustache and
hairy arms.

All in all it was quite an odd gathering. There was the old
landed gentry represented by the Buckleys and Sir Charles'
friends, academia represented by a few of Sebastian's
colleagues and high fashion represented by Serena's crowd.
It was easy to tell which guest belonged to which group. Sir
Charles' male friends' dinner suits were perfectly cut while
their wives' outfits were dominated by expensive jewellery;
Sebastian's colleagues could be spotted by their unkempt
hair and their ungainly walks; Serena's friends, meanwhile,
seemed to be treating the event as a fashion parade. It was
interesting to see them in action. They seemed very different
from the rest of the assembled party, poised and confident
and full of life. It amused me to see them greet each other,
launching into shrieks of welcome before kissing on both
cheeks several times while the older crustier set displayed
little outward emotion.

At about seven-fifteen, Hole announced dinner and led
us through into the state dining room, impressively laid out
with Georgian silver, Sevres chinaware and antique crystal.
Two footmen waited under the butler's command. I was
placed between Belinda and her mother who spent most of
the dinner monopolising Sir Charles, who sat on her other
side.

Belinda's appetite was tremendous. Huge amounts of

food disappeared in complete contrast to poor Nigel sitting opposite. He had drawn the unfortunate position of sitting next to the duchess and his nervousness got worse as the dinner went on. I watched spellbound at one point when a hideous little insect landed on his plate and became stuck in a thick glutinous sauce that accompanied our venison cutlets. His alarm was apparent and obviously not wanting to draw the duchess' attention to the dilemma he hesitated before deciding what to do with it. A few half-hearted attempts to remove it surreptitiously came to nothing and he embarked upon a different and drastic course of action. He ate it.

Belinda didn't seem to do very much at all. Her life seemed to be geared around finding a husband but clearly this was proving more difficult than she had expected. She talked affectionately about her last boyfriend but the more she talked the more she revealed about why they had parted company. Evidently she had not found him at all suitable but, being a pragmatic girl, had devoted her energies to bringing him up to scratch. By the sound of things eventually he had had enough, preferring to go and find himself in India rather than pursue the millions she would inherit.

If Sebastian and Serena were disappointed or dispirited by Sir Charles' eclectic assortment of guests, they certainly didn't show it. Sebastian, usually a reticent conversationalist, was in lively form, and Serena enthralled the colonel and Sir Charles with her assured charm.

I have to admit that I was finding the thing a bit tedious and maliciously hoped for Nigel to provide us with another excitement. Sure enough he didn't fail me. I glanced across at Sophie who had caught on to my train of thought. She smiled furtively.

After we had finished eating, the duchess, in her capacity

as Sir Charles' hostess, stood up to take the ladies through to the Yellow Drawing Room for coffee whilst we stayed behind for port. As the wretched Mr Sicklesmere stood up and gathered his various limbs together into some sort of coherent organisation, he pushed his chair back, gave a little bow to her grace and then abruptly disappeared under the table. There was a sickening thud as he bumped his head against his pudding bowl on the way.

Serena showed the utmost concern and disappeared after him. Assisted by Hole they extricated the librarian who reappeared, slightly dazed, with a quantity of raspberry pavlova mixed in his hair.

'Come,' commanded the duchess, ignoring the fracas, as she gathered the female members of the party. 'The gentlemen will join us later.'

Some kind of order returned to the dining room although the others treated Mr Sicklesmere with a certain coolness. I felt a considerable relief when we finally rejoined the ladies and without too much delay Sophie and I politely took our leave for the evening.

Chapter 24

I had arranged to meet the Smiths at Bull Place Farmhouse to explain that Sebastian and Serena might want to have a look around it. The house was an appropriate choice for them though I doubted the Smiths would think so. Medieval with exposed timbers and, unusually, red-brick in-fill between the beams, it lay in a hollow on the edge of the park and what had once been beautiful formal gardens. The farmland had been amalgamated into a neighbouring farm some years before so it had left the house redundant. A series of short-term tenants had lived in it ever since although the Smiths had stayed for nearly three years. Its chequered history meant that whilst structurally sound the house was tired and needed modernising.

The Smiths wouldn't want to leave but they had no choice under the terms of their tenancy. The ideal solution would be to find them somewhere else on the estate to their liking, and I had an idea that might appeal. They were, to put it mildly, an unusual couple which was probably why they liked the seclusion of the house. Mr Smith, a tall, lean man in his sixties was a recluse. He sported the longest beard I had ever seen – long, white and pointed, he'd once told me that he hadn't cut it for thirty years. He tended to dribble a bit when he talked which made me wonder what sort of things might live in it. Insects probably, some small rodents possibly, mustard and cress almost certainly. A writer, he was a very successful author of creepy books about the occult. Any visits I made tended to be elevenish as I felt there was unlikely to be anything sinister going on mid-morning. Mrs Smith was just as peculiar but in a very different way. For a start she was about thirty, had striking features and long jet black hair. She was beautiful in a menacing, frightening sort of way. She was also a writer, of erotic literature. I had read one of her books and although not a prude, I wondered what on earth inspired her scenarios and characters.

Mrs Smith answered the door and led us through to the kitchen. Mr Smith was seated in a wooden armchair by an old Aga, dribbling into his beard.

'It's kind of you to see me at such short notice,' I said, 'but I wanted to let you know of some possible developments before you heard about them from someone else.'

The combination of their dubious, somewhat sinister interests immediately crossed my mind. The raven-haired beauty had the same blood-coloured fingernails and lips as the walls. She was definitely scary, her dark eyes bored into me as though she was about to pounce, her scarlet talons ripping through my flesh before gutting me like a dead rabbit in the sink. I shook myself back to reality and continued.

'Sebastian Buckley is, as you may already have heard, getting married shortly and it is possible that we may require this house for him and his new wife.'

I waited for some startling reaction and although I thought I detected some movement in Mr Smith's beard, nothing else happened.

'Nothing's definite yet,' I continued, 'but I thought it only fair to let you know as soon as possible. I should know later this week and if you wouldn't mind I'd like to show them the house tomorrow.'

Mrs Smith prised herself away from the sink where she had been leaning and looked at her husband.

'This is a bit of a shock,' she said. 'We love this place. It's just what we need and I'd be reluctant to move. I know we don't have much say in the matter though.'

'I understand that, Mrs Smith,' I replied sympathetically, 'which is why when you first took it on I did mention that it was always a house we might need back. That was the reason it was let on a short-term tenancy.'

The beard moved again very definitely, and I thought I saw a field mouse poking its head out until I realised it was Mr Smith's finger.

'Well bugger it,' he exclaimed and resumed stroking the beard.

'I do have a possible alternative,' I offered, 'providing you don't mind isolation.'

'We crave isolation,' cried Mrs Smith, throwing her arms open wide in a gesture of embrace. 'Where is it?'

'It's old Keeper's Cottage in the middle of Hall Wood. It's much smaller than this and we'd have to do it up a bit, but certainly go and have a look if you want.'

Suddenly the old man leapt up.

'I know it,' he shouted, 'it's perfect, Anastasia, perfect.'

'Take me,' she uttered dramatically, which was a phrase I daresay she used often enough in her books.

I ended up taking them over in the Land Rover as the track to it was pretty rough and unused. Anastasia, which suited her far better than Mrs Smith, sat in the middle seat, her thighs straddling the gear knob. I had felt that it was better if the beard remained near the window in case it, or something in it, needed to get out in a hurry. Land Rovers are not the most decorous of vehicles to drive and I nervously fiddled between Anastasia's thighs to change gear. She however did not display any kind of nerves at all. Possibly she was composing a scene for her next novel.

Fortunately they were enchanted by the cottage, which had all the makings of a setting for either of their books. Totally isolated in a clearing in the wood it had been built as a type of grotto. It had a thatched roof which overhung the walls, supported by rough sawn logs in a rustic fashion. Gothic-style windows poked from the thatch and a massive ornate chimney rose through the centre of the building. Its spooky appearance, coupled with its remote situation, had made it impossible to let. Their willingness to move there could not have been more opportune. If Sebastian wanted Bull Place then two houses could be restored and put to good use.

It was useful to have a plan in mind before the trustees' meeting and as I sat down with them all the following day I felt quietly confident that this was an ideal solution.

Sir Charles, Sebastian and Serena were there together with the three trustees of the estate. The job of the trustees was to ensure that those parts of the estate that had been put in trust for Sebastian were properly administered and I duly sent them reports to keep them updated. In practice the estate was run as Sir Charles dictated and in any case there was only one trustee who mattered, Gordon White. The senior partner of the estate's accountants in London, he had a razor-sharp mind when it came to financial planning.

The other two were more typical of estate trustees. Lord Cocker and the Honourable Mrs Mildred Bassington were old family friends who, like the Buckleys, owned estates and knew how to enjoy them. They were both quite elderly, of Sir Charles' generation, and I am certain that neither of them ever read a word of my reports. They never seemed to know what I was talking about and his lordship compounded the problem by repeatedly digressing from the subject in hand to reminisce over some event with which he had been involved. It had already started.

'So,' I said, 'we need the trustees' approval to allow our agricultural tenant, Fred Bloworth, to put up a new straw yard building for his fattening pigs.'

'I don't think that's such a good idea,' commented the Honourable Mrs Bassington. 'I think there's so much Danish bacon about there's not much point.'

'Our tenant keeps pigs on contract,' I explained, 'and although you are of course right about the Danes, there is still a good living to be made from . . .'

'Used to keep pigs meself,' butted in Lord Cocker. I assume that what he actually meant was that he employed someone who kept pigs for him. I couldn't imagine his lordship in a boiler suit scraping out dung passages. 'Course, very different then,' he went on, 'and we fed 'em swill. Great boilers of the stuff we had. Terrible pong, but used up all the waste.'

'Yes, sir,' I said before he got carried away. 'Of course it's not often practical to feed swill nowadays. These pig contracts are set up by the feed companies who provide the pigs and the feed. It's a low-risk business for Mr Bloworth.'

His lordship snorted loudly and banged his fist down on the table in a gesture of amusement.

'Used to cycle down to the pig farm sometimes,' he guffawed, 'and watch 'em being fed. You've never seen such a mad rush for a trough of food as those pigs. Little blighters they were.'

'I didn't know you'd kept pigs, Crispin,' remarked Mrs Bassington. 'That must have been a while ago.'

'Yes, gave 'em up in '63, I think it was. Pity really, as the muck's so good for the soil. We miss that.'

'Everything is chemical now, isn't it? I mean on the farmland,' she said. 'Such a shame the old ways are dying out. They were very much better in many respects you know. Healthier I think.'

'Mind you, I have to say there was a frightful stink when they were spreading the muck,' offered his lordship. 'Don't miss that!'

Gordon White was looking across the table at me with a blank expression on his face.

'Well, if we could move on, I assume therefore that the trustees approve item four,' he said, 'and more importantly we can now discuss the possibility of a house for Sebastian and Serena'

Gordon White and I had already talked about item four, Mr Bloworth's building, and he was happy with the financial aspects of the proposal. However, no one had even thought about finding Sebastian somewhere to live on the estate. I outlined my ideas concerning Bull Place and Keeper's Cottage, both of which belonged to the trust, and was met with unanimous approval, subject to Sebastian and Serena's agreement.

'Jolly good idea, Sebastian,' blurted out the Honourable Mrs Bassington. 'Time you had a place here you know.' It set Lord Cocker off on another of his digressions.

'When I first went back to Endsleigh' – his family estate – 'my father wanted me to live in the stables.'

'Presumably they were converted?' Gordon White asked.

'Oh, of course,' his lordship went on.'Not a bad place as it happened but right outside his back door. In those days I was a bit of a gadabout, you know, liked to have the ladies round, what.' He chuckled heartily. 'Wanted a bit of privacy.'

Mrs Bassington looked a bit shocked. 'Really, Crispin,' she said.

'Ended up having a bit of a row about it actually. Had to stand my ground until I got a farmhouse like you're suggesting to Sebastian here. I think it's a jolly good idea, jolly good.'

I arranged to take Sebastian and Serena around after lunch and slipped away to telephone the Smiths.

Trustees meetings' always ended before luncheon and then Sir Charles would entertain them to a splendid meal in the formal dining room. We had once tried to continue business afterwards but the Honourable Mrs Bassington had become rather giggly and said some outrageous things and Lord Cocker had become so engrossed in his stories that nothing was achieved. Accordingly, Gordon White had asked me to set agendas that finished by one o'clock.

Chapter 25

Sebastian and Serena were a little shocked by the state of the house and greatly so by the Smiths. Sebastian did not have much imagination when it came to houses and all he could see was its dilapidation, gaudy decoration and overgrown gardens. Serena however, wandered around not saying much but looking thoughtful.

'It's a bit of a mess, James,' he said when the Smiths were out of earshot. 'To be quite honest I would've thought we could find somewhere better than this.'

'As it stands, I agree,' I replied, 'but imagine what could be done. In essence it is a very fine old building, plenty of room and the opportunity to really make something of it. Why don't we walk round and look at the possibilities?'

We went on a tour of the house and I suggested where new bathrooms could be installed, rooms enlarged and layouts changed. Serena became quite enthusiastic and started talking about colour schemes and furnishings.

'We'd talk through all sorts of possibilities,' I explained, 'have an architect draw up plans until you get something you really want.'

'Would we be able to remove say, this wall here?' asked Serena, indicating a division between two small bedrooms.

'I don't know but I expect so,' I said. 'We will be limited by some structural basics that can't be changed and by planning consents as it's a listed building, but by and large

I expect we could do most of the things you'd want to do. This wall doesn't seem structural for instance, so it could probably come out.'

The Smiths were loitering in the kitchen, kindly leaving us to explore the house without their interference. It seemed impolite to discuss possible alterations in front of them but I wanted to explain my thoughts on how the dark, blood-red room could be opened up into a light, airy space by incorporating the disused service rooms adjoining it.

'Won't you be sad to be leaving here?' asked Serena. 'I feel as though we'd be pushing you out.'

'Mr Aden has offered us Keeper's Cottage instead,' replied Anastasia. 'In many ways we'd prefer that to this. We love isolation you see.'

'They're both writers,' I explained, 'so peace is essential to their work.'

Serena then inevitably asked them what kind of books they wrote and for a moment I was worried that she would not be impressed by occult and eroticism.

'Mystery and romance,' Anastasia answered tactfully, 'but not mainstream. I doubt you will have heard of our books.'

Bit of a surprise if she had, I thought.

'Shall we look around the gardens,' I suggested, 'and get out of the Smiths' way.'

Sebastian and Serena made their farewells to the Smiths and we wandered out into the garden. Despite its unkempt state the original layout was obvious. Remnants of stone terraces, yew hedges, a walled kitchen garden, smashed glasshouses and red-brick paths under archways all provided evidence of a former glory.

'You see, we could get all this put right,' I said, it's a fantastic garden. Dredge the pond, which is silted up, relay the driveway, it really would be quite stunning, you know.'

Apart from the fact that I genuinely felt that this was the best available house on the estate for them, I was becoming enthusiastic about the project. There was something challenging and positive about taking on a ruin and transforming it into an architectural gem.

We walked back to the Land Rover, they having arrived by taxi again, when Sebastian said, 'What do you think, Serena?'

She took a long time answering, looking around her with a studious gaze.

'I think this could be beautiful, a wonderful place to bring up children. But I would like it to be ready before the child is born.'

'Well, we can probably get the house ready by then. The gardens might take a bit longer though,' I interjected.

'In that case I think we should say yes to it.' She smiled.

Sebastian looked at me.

'There we are then, we'll come here.'

'Excellent,' I cried, pleased for them. 'I really think you've made a good decision. If we work closely together on the details you'll have just what you want.'

'You'll need to get Keeper's Cottage done first and the Smiths moved out presumably before anything can happen here.'

'Yes, that's true,' I agreed, 'though that shouldn't take too long. We'll have to rush things through a bit here I suppose but we shouldn't need to cut too many corners.'

I think I was more excited than they were. Serena would, I had no doubt, get involved with the plans and have ideas but Sebastian's only passion seemed to be his work. He could be frustrating – sometimes it seemed as though the wealth, the estate and the family heritage all washed over him. I wondered if Serena's arrival into his life had been like that -she just happened to be in the right place at the right time. Or had she provoked a hidden passion.

The CB radio was crackling away in the Land Rover and I could just make out Anne's voice calling me. The installation of the CB radio, which had been approved long before my arrival on the estate, had been a giant leap forward by the previous agent. It supposedly meant that the office could contact me when I was out but in reality it was little more than useless. For a start it required an aerial the size of the Eiffel Tower, which was forever getting snapped off by overhanging branches. The thing wobbled around like an epileptic cyclist and frequently threatened to impale low-flying birds. The main disadvantage though, was that it was difficult to find an empty channel on which to communicate. On the main road to the north of the estate was a busy transport café, whose proprietor, apparently called Shirley, was in constant demand by her lorry driver customers. 'Hisss . . . full monty, Shirl . . . Big Dog's coming in ten . . . put 'em down, luv . . . Shirl's ready and waiting for the Big Dog's do . . .' was the sort of nonsense we usually got to hear.

Anne was trying to say something about Sir Charles, or SC as we referred to him on the radio, who had as usual lost one of the poodles.

'Hiss, hiss, silence, pop . . . was it with us?'

I picked up the handset and pressed the button. 'Land Rover calling office,' I said without much hope.

'Hiss . . . crackle . . . Silver tube just drawing alongside Panzer Pete for a coolie.'

Sebastian and Serena looked at me in faint alarm.

'Bloody thing,' I said turning it off. 'You can never hear

her properly. It's supposed to be my contact with the office, not every lorry driver within ten miles. I'll ring her from the Hall when we get back.'

They had decided to take the train to Cambridge and I offered to drive them to the railway station in Bury St Edmunds after reporting back to Sir Charles and the trustees who were no doubt relaxing after their lunch.

We met Hole cycling slowly down the driveway.

'We're missing a dog,' he said without expression. 'We understand that it has been detained in the estate office.'

'Oh, I did hear Anne trying to get hold of me. I'll go down if you like,' I offered.

'I'm afraid Sir Charles and the trustees are anxious to see you before they leave,' he replied, 'otherwise I should have welcomed the offer.' And with that he pedalled off with the air of a long-suffering but devoted servant.

Serena didn't realise that this happened on a regular basis and Sebastian was so used to it that neither of them commented. I did reflect however that the sight of an elderly butler cycling along in his tailcoat chasing after a poodle was something that might change when the two of them , eventually took over the Hall.

The trustees were in fine form awaiting our arrival and enthusiastic about Sebastian's decision. Gordon White had already left for London but Mrs Bassington and Lord Cocker had, so it seemed, enjoyed several circuits of Sir Charles' port. I think Sir Charles was relieved to see us.

'If you're taking these two to the station,' he said to me, 'perhaps you could take Mrs Bassington with you. Lord Cocker's going in the opposite direction.'

'That's perfectly all right,' I agreed, 'although someone will have to sit in the back.'

'Will they?' asked Sir Charles. 'Oh, the Land Rover's

only got three seats of course. I know, take my car but be careful. I'll get Hole to bring it round.'

'He's just gone down to the village, Sir Charles, to fetch one of the dogs.'

'Oh, bugger, yes. Bloody thing went orf again.'

'Well, I can get it if I can find the keys.'

Jolly good then.'

'Er, do you know where the keys are, Sir Charles?'

There was a pause as he thought about it.

'Do you know, I haven't a clue. Hole always brings it round for me you see. One of the maids might know.'

I couldn't find anyone in the servants' quarters so I rang the estate office hoping to catch Hole.

'You're going to drive Sir Charles' motor car,' he repeated in disbelief as if referring to a Rolls-Royce or some equally desirable model.

'Just to the railway station,' I confirmed.

'I've never known anyone drive Sir Charles' motor car before,' he said, 'this is a very rare, no a unique occasion.'

It was also a faintly ridiculous situation. After all it was only an old Morris worth about £300.

'These are Sir Charles' instructions,' I said firmly, 'but he doesn't know where the keys are kept.'

'The key, there is only one, will be found hanging in my office above my desk. It has a label attached describing the vehicle.'

As there was only the one vehicle it seemed an unnecessary precaution. However, Hole was meticulous in his ministrations.

'You will need to engage full choke upon starting the engine,' he kindly explained, 'and reduce this to halfway as you pass the stable archway.'

Hole had never driven any further than the front door

in his life so his instructions ended abruptly at that point. He was no doubt also aware that I had mastered the technicalities of operating a motor vehicle and would be able to proceed without further advice.

By the time I got the thing round to the front door the others were waiting in the porch.

'The car is here, Sir Charles,' I said. The Honourable Mrs Bassington marched unsteadily out the door.

'I think Mildred should ride in the front,' suggested Sir Charles wisely for I doubt she would have been able to squeeze in the back.

'Do take care,' he warned.

'Safe journey, what?' bellowed the peer and with enough ceremony to be reminiscent of the pioneering days of motoring we left on our eight-mile journey to the station.

Sebastian and Serena seemed buoyed up by the events of the day and I sensed, even in Sebastian's usually reticent manner, some excitement. The wedding plans were all in hand and there was a new purpose on the estate. Sir Charles himself had a spring in his step as though a great weight had been lifted off his shoulders. His family would go on.

The Honourable Mrs Bassington was in less good spirits. The after-effects of the port were taking hold and as we weaved a steady but winding way through the Suffolk countryside towards Bury St Edmunds, her face grew whiter and whiter. I tried to distract her by engaging her in conversation but she simply replied 'Tally ho' to all my questions and then wiped the dribble from her chin. When we got to the station I waited to see them off on their respective trains, afraid that she might Well have been found slumped in the waiting room by a passing porter should I have left her.

Chapter 26

'I've no bloody idea how the buggers got out this time, Mr Aden,' lamented Harry Middlemas as he leant on his crook. 'It seems to me they can get through the eye of a needle.'

I was standing by a five-bar gate looking across a field of pasture that should have been full of sheep. Yet there was not one in sight. They had all escaped into a young plantation and were at that very moment devouring our carefully planted hew trees.

Despite the problem I couldn't help but marvel at the joy of my job. It was a beautiful autumn day, with bright sunshine and clear blue skies. The chill in the air was diminishing as the warmth of the sun burnt away the final wisps of mist that lay in the lower folds of the valleys. The trees and hedges were displaying their full autumnal plumage. Reds, golds, yellows, browns and greens in a kaleidoscopic array of nature's colours were changing by the day. For a moment, Mr Middlemas and his sheep were forgotten as I revelled in the amazing beauty of the pastoral landscape before me. There was a row of ancient thatched cottages beside the track behind us, the flint tower of Frampton Church in the distance and the river meandering lazily through the water meadows in the near foreground. It was a timeless picture uninterrupted by cars or the thousands of walkers that made their pilgrimage to this part of the country every year.

Harry Middlemas was smoking a pipe and a great cloud of smoke wafted into my vision, bringing me back to the issue in hand.

'The trouble is, Harry, that your damn sheep are forever getting out. It's become rather a bore and they're beginning to cause quite a lot of damage in these woods.'

'I know, Mr Aden, don't think I don't know. But as I say, it's beyond me how they do it.'

'I'll tell you how they do it, Harry. They take one look at your fences and then walk straight through. They're all rotting away or falling down.'

He looked at me with astonishment. 'I don't know what you mean. There's nothing wrong with me fences.'

'Well let's take a walk around this field then,' I suggested, opening the gate. Unsurprisingly it didn't open very easily. One hinge had broken and been replaced with a length of wire and the fastening catch had disappeared altogether. It was held shut by numerous bits of baler twine so knotted that it was impossible to determine which pieces to untie.

'Here,' Harry said, and reached over to cut it with a well-used pen knife. 'Catch's missing,' he added unnecessarily.

A sheepdog which had been sitting quietly beside him shot through the opening and tore along the side of the field, keeping close to the ground, its eyes searching for his master's sheep. A sharp trill of a whistle brought it abruptly to a halt and it crouched motionless, waiting for a command.

'A good dog that,' commented the farmer through a puff of smoke.

'Now let's look at these hedges, Harry,' I said as we made our way over the field. 'You see they're all gappy and dead underneath and all you've done is shove bits of old wire or whatever in the holes. It's no wonder the sheep keep getting out.'

He muttered something I didn't catch and we continued in silence. I didn't mind a bit. He was a likeable old rogue, the third generation of his family to hold the tenancy of Park Farm and a true and knowledgeable countryman. What he didn't know about the birds, plants and animals on the estate wasn't worth knowing. He had often answered my queries when I had discovered something unusual on my travels.

We reached the hedgeline bordering the new wood and it was immediately obvious where the sheep had escaped. A gap in the bottom of the thorn hedge was covered in wool and a worn track led into the wood.

'That's the place then, Harry,' I said.

'Yup,' he agreed, 'buggers, aren't they?'

We found a place where we could climb through and set off through the young woodland to find the sheep. His dog, every nerve in its shaggy, lithe body alert, crept along the ground some way ahead searching for signs of his charges.

The warmth of the sun was getting stronger, the light brighter and the twittering of the birds louder. The freshness of the pure air was a tonic to inhale, to savour and enjoy. Harry could probably have done the job on his own, but I wouldn't miss it for the world.

'Away to me, Ben,' he suddenly shouted and I heard the rustling of a group of sheep running through the long grass of the plantation. Gradually the flock increased in size until Harry reckoned he had found the lot. Slowly he moved them back to the gap in the hedge and sure enough, once one had spotted it they streamed through, shoving frantically, repeatedly getting stuck when two or more made the dash together.

When they'd all returned, Harry delved into the pockets

of an extraordinarily large and dirty overcoat to produce some lengths of string.

'Don't worry,' he chuckled, looking up at me, 'that's just a temporary measure, not a new fence!'

I laughed. 'At least you've got the message then,' I said, 'but you realise you're going to have to erect a new fence all along this boundary otherwise this is going to keep on happening.'

'God knows how I'll afford it,' he replied. 'This farming job's rock bottom as you well know. Hardly worth keeping these damn things nowadays, more's the pity.' He stood up to relight his pipe. 'You know, Mr Aden,' he went on, 'last week in Bury market there was good cull ewes that didn't make a fiver. A packet of me baccy here costs more than a blooming sheep. It's beyond belief.'

I had to agree with him, farming was in trouble. The state of the rural economy was getting pretty desperate. I was grateful that the size of Sir Charles' estate meant that his farm would be viable for a while yet. But I knew that for people like Harry their way of life was dying. The valuable knowledge and understanding that Harry and his ilk brought to the countryside was being lost and what seemed to be coming in its place was a giant theme park for the benefit of people who lived in and understood the city but knew nothing of working with nature. It was ironic that their professed love for the environment was threatening to make an endangered species like Harry extinct.

Despite the difficulties Harry gave me his word that the fencing would be done and I knew that was as good as or better than any signed piece of paper. Besides there was more than enough paper in my office.

Anne was rushing out as I arrived back.

'I've got to take the cat to the vets,' she explained. 'I'll be back in an hour. Oh, and by the way, Sir Charles would like you to take him down to Bull Place this afternoon.'

I had acted with great speed on the arrangements for converting Bull Place into a home for Sebastian and Serena. They were now anxious to take up residence on the estate as soon as possible. After the initial apparent indifference they had both, Serena particularly, taken a huge interest in the renovations and were visiting as often as they could to monitor the progress. Sir Charles was overjoyed at the prospect of his son and heir, his wife and their imminent addition moving back to Frampton. He had watched the work at the farmhouse with growing impatience and at least once a week I accompanied him down there for a visit.

I rang the Hall and waited as usual for ages. A rather breathless Hole picked up the telephone.

'Frampton Hall,' he stated.

'Morning, Mr Hole, James Aden here. Could I speak to Sir Charles, please?'

'Certainly, Mr Aden. I will try to ascertain his where-abouts and then transfer you,' he said, as though he was operating a telephone switchboard. There was only the one extension in Sir Charles' study and if he wasn't there then it often took Hole ages to find him. In fact this time it only took just under ten minutes.

'I'm sorry to have kept you, Mr Aden,' he gasped, out of breath. 'Sir Charles was out on the south lawn feeding a cock pheasant that's taken a liking to our gardens.'

'Oh, thank you,' I said.

'I'll put you through now, sir.'

There was another considerable delay before the telephone was answered.

'Good morning, Sir Charles, it's James here,' I said.

'It's not Sir Charles, I'm afraid, this is still Hole speaking.'

'Oh, why's that?'

'I seem to be getting no reply from the study. If you'd be so kind as to hold on for just another minute, I'll find out where Sir Charles has gone.'

'Okay,' I agreed, resigned to another ten-minute delay. Hole was back in five.

'Sorry, sir,' he panted and then added in a whisper, 'Sir Charles was indisposed, he's ready now.'

This time I was put through and made the arrangement to collect him at three o'clock. Sir Charles always managed to look distinguished even if, upon close inspection, his clothes were threadbare. He was wandering about on the gravel sweep on the south front of the Hall when I arrived, looking as though he had dropped something. His tall, lean frame, slightly stooped with age, was clad in an immaculately tailored tweed suit, frayed around the collar and cuffs, and a highly polished pair of hand-made brogues. Hole must have polished them thousands of times to have honed them to a deep mahogany colour.

'Good afternoon, Sir Charles,' I greeted him.

'Isn't it lovely?' he said. 'My favourite time of the year this, you know. Just look at; the colours,' and he waved his arm across the rolling vista in front of us. The centuries-old parkland fell away towards the gently rippling waters of the lake, the undulating open countryside spreading out into the far distance suffused with the golden light of autumn sun.

'Hunting's just started,' he continued, 'had some marvellous partridge days. What more could a man want?'

With the massive sprawl of Frampton Hall behind him, his 10,000 acres around him and enough wealth to finance a minor European country, I doubted there was anything more. Except perhaps a new suit.

'Were you searching for something?' I asked, as he began peering at the ground again.

'No, no, haven't lost anything. But what d' you think these are?' he queried, pointing at what appeared to be some rabbit droppings.

'Rabbit droppings,' I suggested.

'Well I'm not so sure,' he said. 'I think it might be deer.'

I looked more carefully. 'Don't you think they're a bit small for deer?'

'Possibly,' he said, 'could be a young deer though.'

'I'll have a word with the gardeners,' I assured him. 'This is supposed to be fenced off. Don't want deer or rabbits, come to that, in the gardens eating the new hedges they've just planted.'

'Exactly my thoughts,' he said. 'Jolly good then, shall we go.'

Sir Charles was delighted with the progress being made at Bull Place. It had been an interesting project renovating the sixteenth-century hall house to its former glory and I had enjoyed overseeing it all. The pond had been dredged and was filling up again with clear water and the gardens were unrecognisable from the state they had been in such a short while ago.

'I'm glad this has worked out so well,' he told me, 'and not simply for Sebastian and Serena.' He paused for a few long moments. 'I don't think it'll be many years, you know, before they should have the Hall. I shall be perfectly content to retire down here then.'

He was as happy as I'd ever known him, inspecting the ongoing work, dreaming perhaps of the secured future of his estate. 'I don't own all this really,' he'd once told me, 'I'm just a life tenant. But I want to be a good guardian of this piece of England before I hand it on. A good guardian.'

He was standing on the terrace beside the pond and I watched him, the eighth baronet Buckley, his rolling acres stretching out to the horizon beyond in the fading light of the afternoon, and was strangely thankful that a man with his integrity controlled such a vast tract of our heritage.

Sir Charles caught me staring at him and mistakenly assumed that I'd noticed, as he just had, that his flies were undone. Fastening them without a hint of embarrassment, he commented, 'Nothing to worry about there. A dead bird never falls out of its nest!'

I laughed. 'Actually, Sir Charles, talking of nests, that reminds me. I've been meaning to tell you. Sophie's expecting a baby in the spring.'